There are instructions for one fairy and one butterfly. The same will apply to the other patterns provided. You can mix and match wings and bodies.

Instructions are provided for making these into pins, the same basic intructions apply to all. You can also make these into necklaces, barrettes, bolos, ornaments, or whatever.

Fringe is always your option, I tell you what I have done but you should venture out and try new fringe to make each fairy unique.

The butterfly type fairy wings can also be made into butterflies. See butterfly instructions and patterns (Pg. 20).

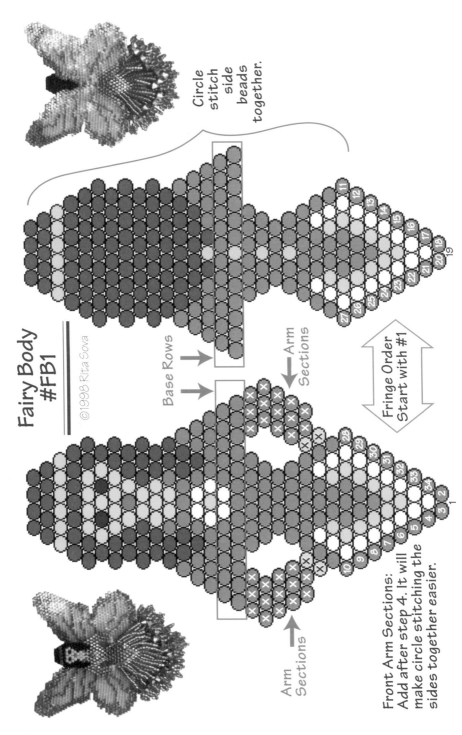

Fairy Body
#FB1

©1998 Rita Sova

Circle stitch side beads together.

Base Rows

Arm Sections

Fringe Order
Start with #1

Arm Sections

Front Arm Sections:
Add after step 4. It will
make circle stitching the
sides together easier.

2

Fairy: Use the brick stitch to make 1 front & 1 back Fairy section.

With wrong sides together:

1. Stitch the top 4 hair beads of front & back together.
2. Circle/peyote stitch the back to the front along one side, only beads shown in bracket. Do not include lower dress section. (The arm section of the front will not be included. Follow along back section and match beads to front section only.)
3. Cut a 2" x 2" section of stuffing (panty hose or a knee high).
4. While circle/peyote stitching the other side of your Fairy together, stuff as you go. Try to catch small parts of stuffing while stitching, this will keep stuffing in place.
5. Add front arm sections.
6. Add fringe to the skirt, front and back.

Fringe: I used a 9-1-6 (last 5 = turnaround) pattern. Start from the bottom center (down bead on right, add 9 purple, 1-4 mm gold - 6 purple beads, go up 1st of last 6 added and continue up all remaining fringe beads and bead on left of brick stitch section). On the other (except bottom center) fringe you will follow above except, insert needle into same bead thread is coming out of on brick stitch section.

3

Fairy Wings #FWM1

Wings: x = Common beads of Fairy Back and wings

1. Make 2 wing sections.
2. The x marked beads are where to attach the wings to the Fairy's back section. Stitch 1 wing to the back now.
3. Attach the other wing section to the back and make very secure.
4. Optional: Use a circle stitch to attach the Fairy's arm to a wing. I attach the widest elbow bead to a wing bead. Attach on both sides. Or, circle stitch the hands together and add a flower or ? in her hands.

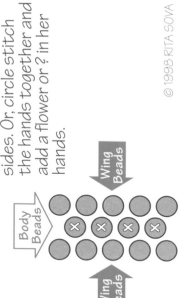

Make 2 separate wing sections.

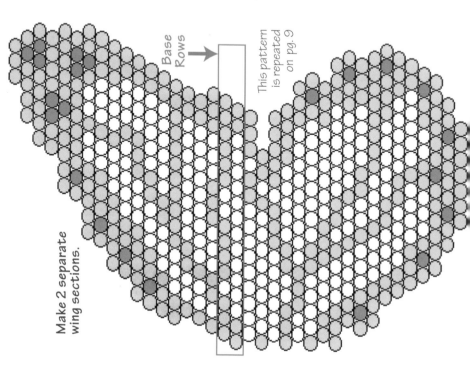

Base Rows →

This pattern is repeated on pg. 9

4

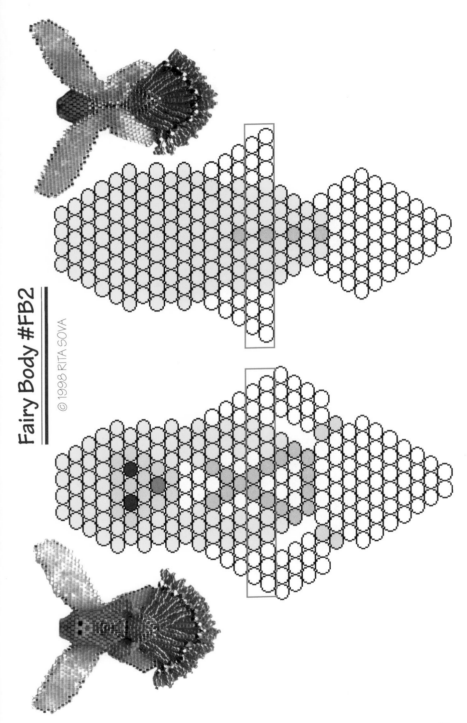

Fairy Body #FB2

Fairy Body #FB3

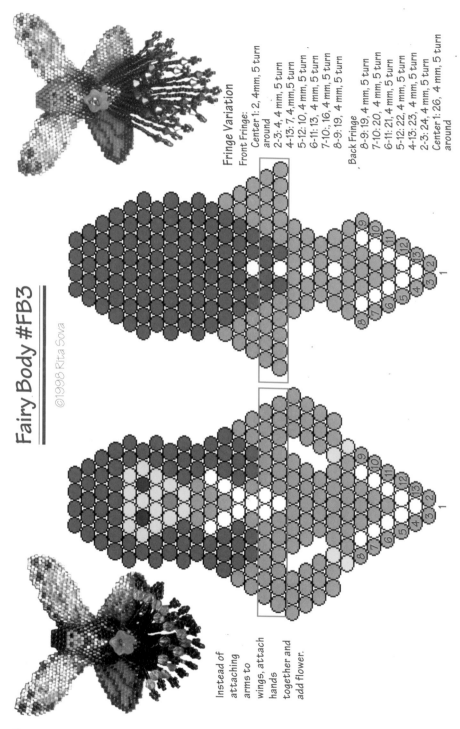

Instead of attaching arms to wings, attach hands together and add flower.

Fringe Variation

Front Fringe:

Center 1: 2, 4mm, 5 turn around
2-3: 4, 4 mm, 5 turn around
4-13: 7, 4,mm,5 turn
5-12: 10, 4 mm, 5 turn
6-11:13, 4 mm, 5 turn
7-10:, 16, 4 mm, 5 turn
8-9: 19, 4 mm, 5 turn

Back Fringe

8-9:19, 4 mm, 5 turn
7-10: 20, 4 mm, 5 turn
6-1: 21, 4 mm, 5 turn
5-12: 22, 4 mm, 5 turn
4-13: 23, 4 mm, 5 turn
2-3: 24, 4 mm, 5 turn
Center 1: 26, 4 mm, 5 turn around

Fairy Body #FB4

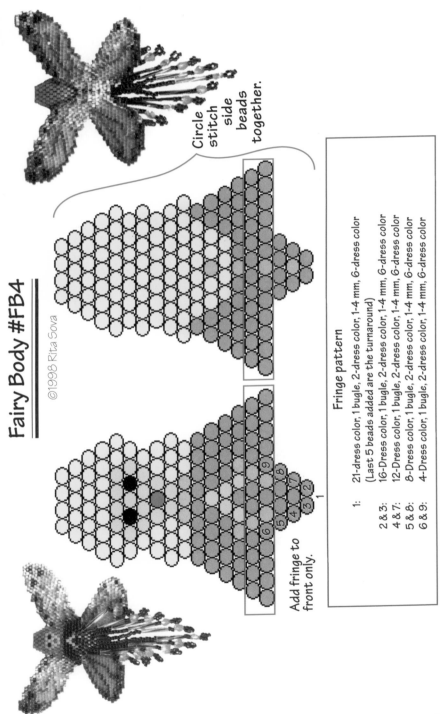

Circle stitch side beads together.

Add fringe to front only.

Fringe pattern

1: 21-dress color, 1 bugle, 2-dress color, 1-4 mm, 6-dress color
(Last 5 beads added are the turnaround)

2 & 3: 16-Dress color, 1 bugle, 2-dress color, 1-4 mm, 6-dress color

4 & 7: 12-Dress color, 1 bugle, 2-dress color, 1-4 mm, 6-dress color

5 & 8: 8-Dress color, 1 bugle, 2-dress color, 1-4 mm, 6-dress color

6 & 9: 4-Dress color, 1 bugle, 2-dress color, 1-4 mm, 6-dress color

Fairy Body #FB5

©1998 Rita Sova

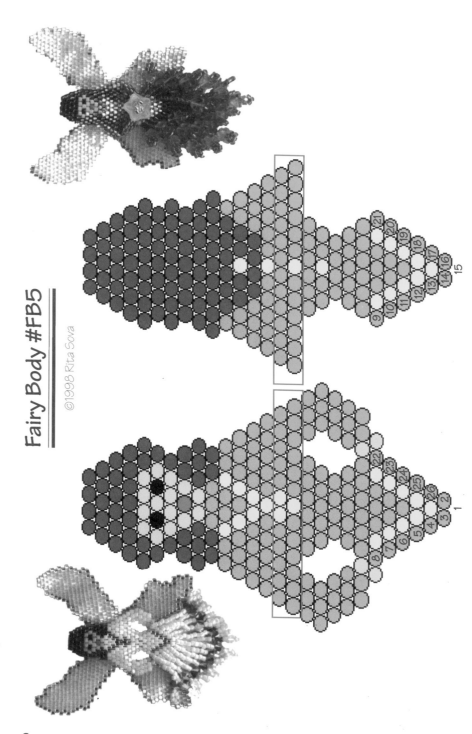

Butterfly (Medium) or Fairy Wings

#FWM1 (Repeat)

Butterfly (Medium) or Fairy Wings

#FW01

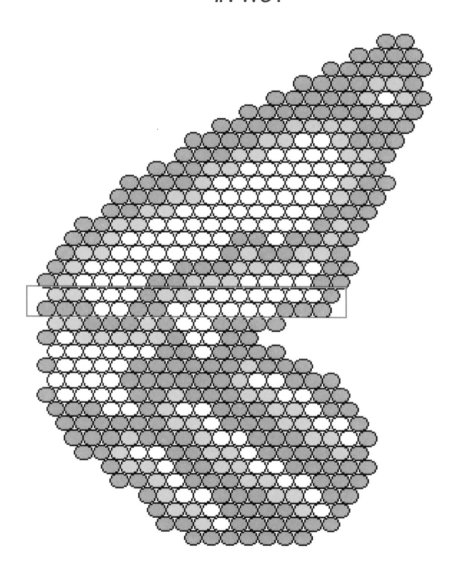

Butterfly (Medium) or Fairy Wings

#FWP1

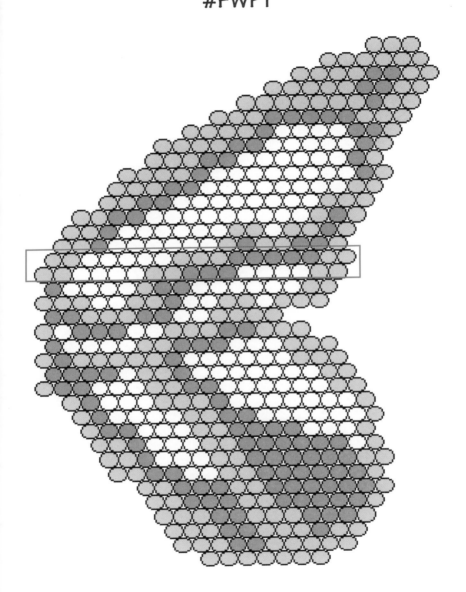

Fairy Wings #FW1

Fairy Wings #FW2

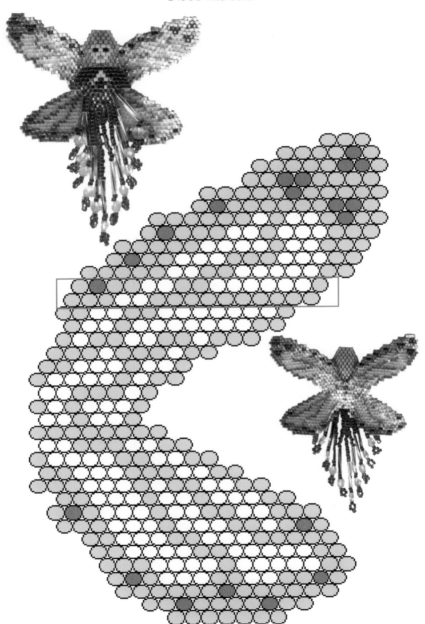

Fairy Wings #FW3

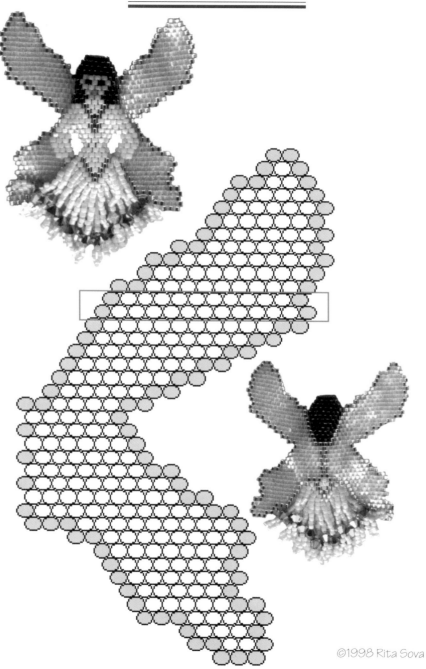

Fairy Wings #FW4

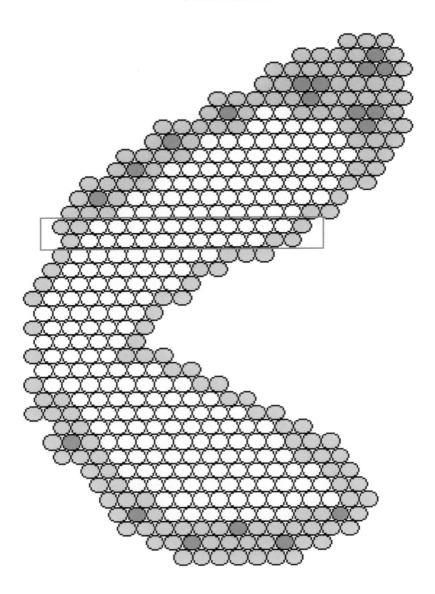

15

Fairy Wings #FW5

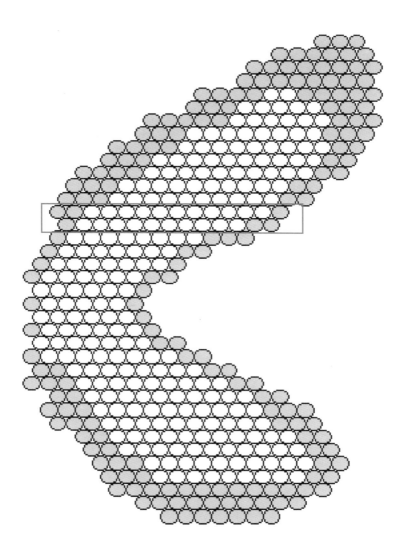

Fairy Wings #FW6

©1998 Rita Sova

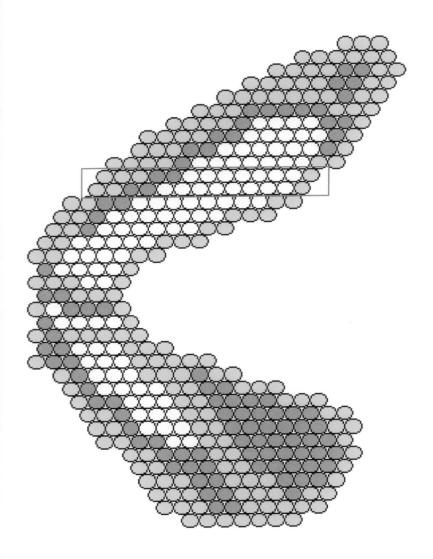

Fairy Wings #FW7

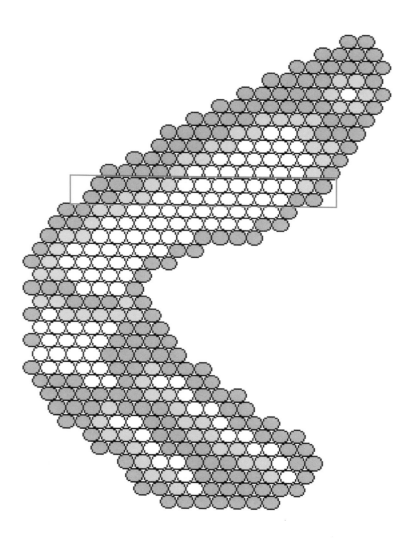

Monarch Butterfly Pattern #M1

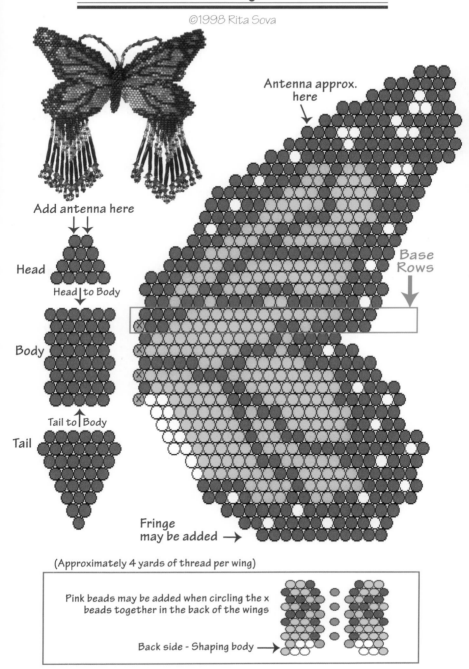

Antenna approx. here

Add antenna here

Head

Head to Body

Body

Tail to Body

Tail

Base Rows

Fringe may be added →

(Approximately 4 yards of thread per wing)

Pink beads may be added when circling the x beads together in the back of the wings

Back side - Shaping body →

19

Butterfly Instructions

1. Brick Stitch 2 wing sections.

2. Add body shown above to both wings (1 body attached to 2 wings).

3. Add head and tail sections to body. Head and tail do not connect to the wings.

4. Body/head/tail must be shaped. Fold body in half, pinch wings together at body to make body rounded. Choose which beads on the back side of wings to stitch together to form the desired shape (I usually use the beads marked x), you may have to add beads here and there to fill in the bare spots. Try using a bugle bead to stuff the body to help hold its shape. Great fun, you must be imaginative.

5. Don't forget the antenna. I use thread (not wire) 3-4 threads through each antenna.

6. Attach to desired medium: barrette, pin back, hair comb, or add chains to make a wonderful necklace.

7. Sometimes clear nail polish is needed to stiffen the wings. Always try a test spot first.

Rita's Butterfly Pattern #01

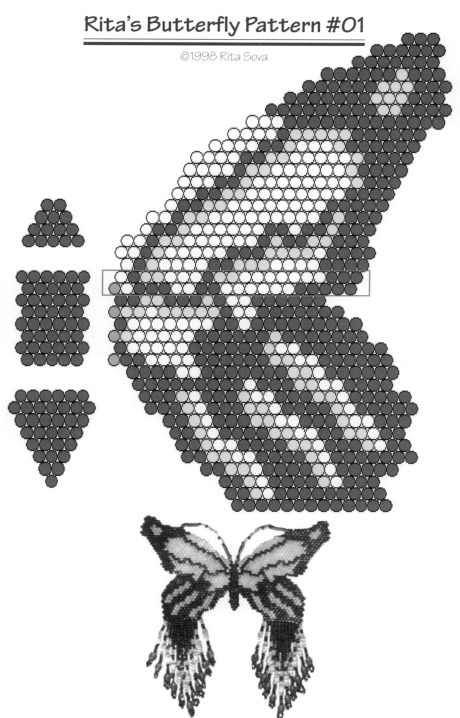

Rita's Butterfly Pattern #02

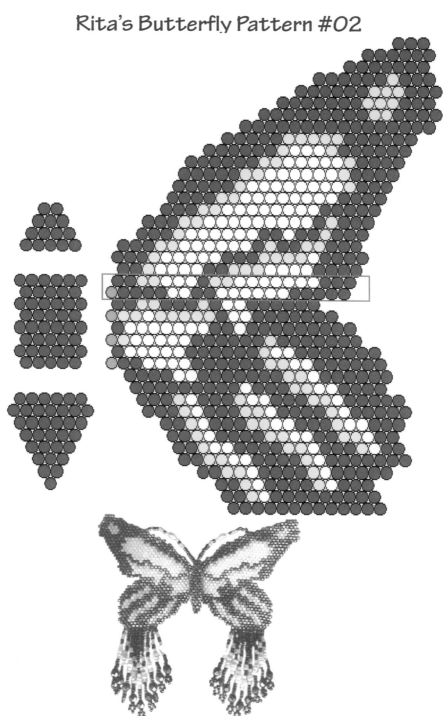

Painted Butterfly Pattern #P1

©1998 Rita Sova

Painted Butterfly Pattern #P2

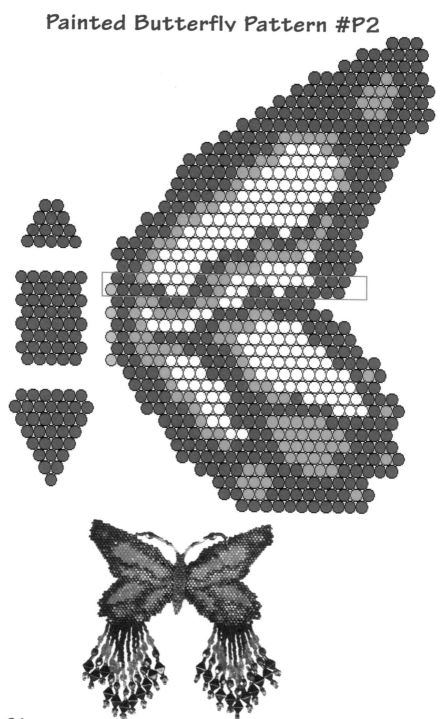

Monarch Necklace

Chain: Round peyote, 6-bead circle
Monarch: Delica Beads

Gift to Sylvia, Santa Fe, NM

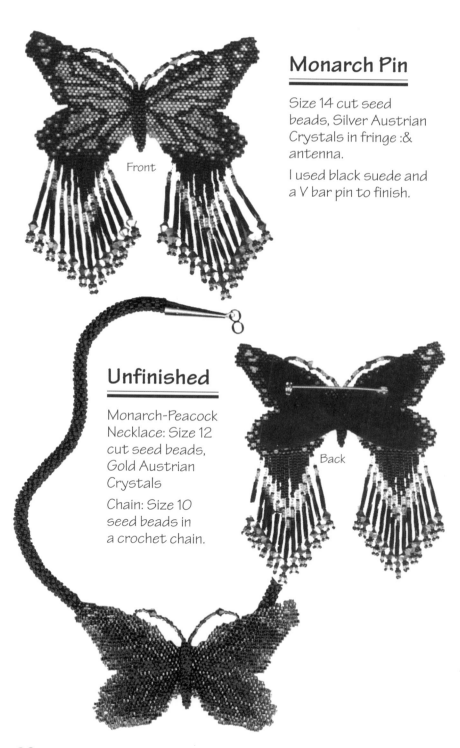

Monarch Pin

Size 14 cut seed beads, Silver Austrian Crystals in fringe :& antenna.

I used black suede and a V bar pin to finish.

Front

Unfinished

Monarch-Peacock Necklace: Size 12 cut seed beads, Gold Austrian Crystals

Chain: Size 10 seed beads in a crochet chain.

Back

BRICK STITCH INSTRUCTIONS

Basic Rules for Butterfly or Fairy Patterns:

1. Read all material and check supplies before beginning.

2. You will not tie knots. To end or start new threads you will weave; in, out, back & forth, beads until thread is secure. Thread should not be showing between or over beads. Then thread may be cut.

3. I try to start with enough thread so I don't have to add, but sometimes plans fall through. Usually 1/2 for top section and 1/2 for the bottom section. Thread is not doubled.

4. Put your pattern into a clear protective sheet and use an erasable marker to keep track of where you are, you can reuse patterns again & again.

5. The use of wax or thread conditioners is optional; these products make your thread easier to handle (among other things). Wax is optional on small projects but required on larger ones. Anything thread can find to wrap around, including itself, it will.

6. Patterns are read in a zigzag fashion. Base row(s)=left to right, row 2=right to left, row 3=left to right, etc. Sometimes you will need to turn the pattern upside down to see your beginning triangle.

7. Instructions are written from a right hander's point of view. I hold the beads between my left thumb and forefinger and the needle in my right hand. I always work from left to right (reading pattern is still done in a zigzag fashion.) You will have to adjust your direction if you hold work other than described.

Up: the needle point is pointing in the up direction.
Down: needlepoint is pointing in the down direction.

Circle stitch example: Thread is coming out of the top of a bead: Pick up one bead, insert needle up through the bead the thread is coming out of, snug. Insert needle down bead just added.

2 Bead Base Row Technique

2 rows of beads at a time, faster for Delica or seed bead base rows.

Do not let go of the triangle made in step 1 while adding the 2 beads in step 2.
Only snug beads after the second stitch in step 2 is completed.
To snug the beads, pull the thread up and slightly to the left.

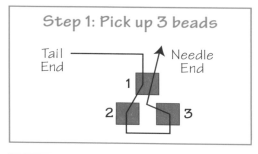

Step 1: Pick up 3 beads

Tail End — Needle End

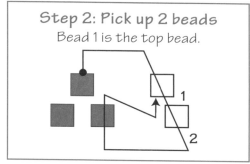

Step 2: Pick up 2 beads
Bead 1 is the top bead.

Step 1: Read pattern left to right for base row. Pick up 3 beads, insert needle into bead 1 to form a triangle as shown. Use thumb and forefinger to hold these beads in place while doing step 2, if you let go 99% of the time you must just start over.

Step 2: This is a 2 stitch process do not snug bead until the second stitch is completed.

1st stitch of step 2: Pick up 2 beads, (1st bead picked up is the top bead), keep thread in back of needle and insert needle up into bead 3 of the triangle, pull gently.

2nd stitch of step 2: With thread in front of the needle, insert needle up into bead 1 just added and snug up, you should have 2 beads on top and 3 beads on bottom. (You can let go of the tringle now.)

Repeat step 2 to the end of the base row.

Complete base row before beginning Brick stitch section. Row 2 - read pattern right to left. Make sure you are watching your pattern for correct color placement.

Brick Stitch

1. Pick up 2 beads, insert needle under the loop of thread between beads, skip loop 1. Insert needle under loop 2 (needle pointing toward you (going from back to front)). Snug beads and thread.

Stitch shown: Green - red - blue.

(⌒ = Loops)

Insert needle up through the last bead added, (bead not on the end), snug up, this will make it stand on end. * Insert needle down through the 1st of the 2 beads added (bead on the end) and back up through the 2nd bead (bead not on the end),* Your thread is coming out of the 2nd bead ready to add the third), * to* = a circle stitch.

(Thread is shown in Blue)

Snug beads into place. Both beads should stand on end and be secure.

2. Pick up 1 bead, insert needle under next loop. Snug gently. Insert needle up through the bead just added and snug. (Too tight and work is rigid, too loose and work is sloppy.)

3. Repeat step 2 to the end.

If your thread is pulled too tightly your work will become very rigid and many times warped. Try to relax, just pull up slack without yanking. Your completed work will be more flexible and smoother to the touch. This is very important.

Continue using the steps above for the brick stitch.

Increase & Decrease

Increasing - beginning of row:

Pick up 2 beads as always at the beginning of the row. Instead of inserting needle under the second loop of thread you will insert needle under 1st loop of thread, and snug. Insert needle up through the last bead added and snug, (1st bead added with shift left and be your increase). Insert needle down through the 1st of the 2 beads added and back up through the 2nd bead (you are just doing a circle stitch around the two beads, you will be coming out of the 2nd bead ready to add the third).

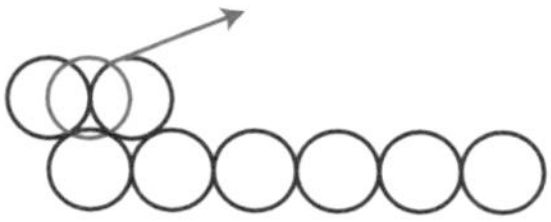

- To increase more than one bead at the beginning of the row: do steps shown above, then use the circle stitch.

Increasing - end of row:

When all beads are added for this row except the increase beads: your thread will be coming out of the last bead added: Add 1 bead, go up through the last bead added and snug, insert needle down into the bead to the left of the bead your thread is coming out of, snug. Insertneedle into a bead in the row below at an angle, snug. Insert needle up one bead to the right of bead thread is coming out of and up into row above and out of bead just increased. (Its like a maze you must weave through beads so your thread doesn't show to get where you want to be - ready for the next bead.)

- To increase more than one bead at the end of the row: use the circle stitch.

Decreasing - Beginning of Row:

Example: Your thread is coming out of bead 1; you must reposition the thread to be coming out of bead   . Insert needle down into bead 2, down into bead in row below (bead 2), up into bead on the side (bead 3) (also in row below), and up into bead 2 of top row. Plan your route before starting, it is difficult to take out this thread. Add 2 beads at the beginning of your row as usual.

Decreasing - End of Row: Stop and turn to start next row, and/or, Position needle coming out of desired bead.

Finishing Work:

I have made these into pins for this book, but I have also made them into necklaces, and barrettes.

Follow the instructions on page 32, to make these into pins.

Use your imagination to make them into barrettes or necklaces.

Have fun!

Finishing items into Pins:

- Chose the size pin you want to use.
- I like to cover the backside of the metal pin with suede/pigskin. Cut a piece of soft suede or pigskin to a desirable shape, make sure there is enough to cover the pin back.
- Where ever you are going to use glue, I recommend you paint that area with clear nail polish (I use a base/topcoat) Use a medium amount of polish on the backside of item - always do a test spot first - some dyed beads will bleed, sometimes weird things happen. There is something about the nail polish that helps the glue adhere to the beads better.
- If needed cut slits or make a hole in the suede using an awl. Insert your pin and check position.
- Apply glue to the backside of the suede/pigskin and position over beads and press/smooth into place. (I like BOND 527)
- Let dry overnight. Keep in mind that however the item is positioned is the shape it will have when the glue is dry. Lay flat or prop into desired shape.

Movers, Shakers and Players

Stage 3
18-24 months

Movers, Shakers and Players

ISBN 1-905019-52-1

© Featherstone Education Ltd, 2006
Text © Clare Beswick and Sally Featherstone, 2006
Illustrations © Martha Hardy, 2005
Series Editor, Sally Featherstone

First published in the UK, January 2006

Published in the United Kingdom by
Featherstone Education Ltd
44 - 46 High Street
Husbands Bosworth
Leicestershire
LE17 6LP

'Little Baby Books'
is a trade mark of
Featherstone
Education Ltd

Printed in Malta on paper produced in the European Union from managed, sustainable forests

Movers, Shakers and Players

Birth to Three Matters

Stage 3
18 to 24 months

Written by Clare Beswick and Sally Featherstone

Illustrated by Martha Hardy

A *Little Baby* Book
Published by Featherstone Education

Featherstone Education

About Little Baby Books

A Strong Child
Me, myself and I
A sense of belonging
Being acknowledged & affirmed
Developing self assurance

A Skilful Communicator
Being together
Finding a voice
Listening & responding
Making meaning

A Competent Learner
Being imaginative
Being creative
Making Connections
Representing

A Healthy Child
Growing and developing
Keeping safe
Making healthy choices
Emotional wellbeing

Birth to Three Matters (DfES SureStart 2002) the Framework for Effective Practice with Babies and Very Young Children, sends a clear and unequivocal message underlining the importance of home and family working together with practitioners to lay the best possible foundations for life and learning. The Guidance recognises and celebrates the individuality of babies and young children, providing a wealth of guidance and support to those with responsibility for their care and education.

The first series of Little Baby Books was published in 2003 to build on the principles of the guidance and provide practical handbooks, with a collection of easy-to-follow ideas and activities for babies and young children from birth to three. The first series has been expanded to sixteen books, each linked and colour coded to one of the aspects of the Framework, and each offering activities for each of the developmental stages.

These four aspects of the Framework are:
* A Strong Child (Purple Books)   * A Skilful Communicator (Pink Books)
* A Competent Learner (Green Books) * A Healthy Child (Blue Books)

All the activities in the Baby Books use objects and resources readily available in homes and settings. They allow babies and children to develop at their own pace, to make unhurried discoveries and allow for much repetition as well as trying out of new ideas. This encourages young children to become increasingly independent, making their own choices. All the activities require the careful and skilful support of an adult. The role of the adult is included in the step-by-step 'What you do' section.

Stages of Development

<u>Birth to Three Matters (DfES SureStart 2002) the Framework</u>, uses 'headings to describe children at four developmental stages'. These headings describe children at differing stages of development, linked to broad bands of age.

Young babies from birth to 8 months - **described as** 'Heads up Lookers and Communicators'
Babies from 8 to 18 months - **described as** 'Sitters, Standers and Explorers'
Young children from 18 to 24 months - **described as** 'Movers, Shakers and Players'
Children from 24 to 36 months - **described as** 'Walkers, Talkers and Pretenders'.

Practitioners are encouraged to look carefully at the babies and children in their groups and decide which heading describes these children best. Observations of the children you work with may mean that you refer to the activities for children at an earlier or later stage. This may apply to a whole range of children, including:

babies and children with special or additional needs
babies and children whose home language is not English
babies and children whose development is delayed or more advanced
babies and children who need more experience in a particular component or aspect
children who are new to your setting and need confidence while settling in.

These four new Baby Book collections have been published at the request of practitioners and settings, so the activities can be available in each room. We suggest that you may wish to use the two most relevant books in each room, as this will probably match the broad range of development you work with. However, we also advise you to refer to the whole series when planning experiences for children whose development is delayed or more advanced.

young babies
0-8 months
Heads up lookers and communicators

babies
8-18 months
Sitters, standers and explorers

young children
18-24 months
Movers, shakers and players

children
24-36 months
Walkers, talkers and pretenders

Heads up Lookers and communicators

Stage 1

Sitters, Standers and Explorers

Stage 2

Movers, Shakers and Players

Stage 3

Walkers, Talkers and Pretenders

Stage 4

The Little Baby Books in Stages

These Baby Books are a reorganisation of the material in the original series of 16 Baby Books. They have just been divided in a different way!

Sixteen books have become four books, organised by developmental stage:

	Stage 1	Heads up Lookers and Communicators (Young Babies 0 to 8 months)
This book →	Stage 2	Sitters, Standers and Explorers (Babies 8 to 18 months)
	Stage 3	Movers, Shakers and Players (Young Children 18 to 24 months)
	Stage 4	Walkers, Talkers and Pretenders (Children 24 to 36 months).

Each book contains the activities for each developmental stage, with sections for each aspect and each component. It is for practitioners to decide which stage best meets the needs of the children in their care, and whether to use these books, presented by developmental stage or the original set of sixteen which are presented by Aspect and Component.

The experiences suggested in this book will help young children to grow and develop through a range of planned and informal activities, many of which will be familiar to you. The activities use objects and resources easily available in most homes and settings, they focus on practical activities and purposeful play for individuals, pairs and very small groups. They will help babies to develop positive relationships and trust as they play and learn with adults and other children.

Each activity page gives step-by-step instructions, tips, plenty of further ideas for children ready for more, practical ideas on differentiation for babies with special needs, as well as tips on what to look and listen for.

With ideas for home links, 'Little Baby Books in Stages' continue to give practical support to ensure parents and practitioners are working together to nurture the development and wellbeing of young children.

Watch, listen, reflect

Assessing young children's learning is a difficult process, but we do know that any assessment must be based on careful observation of children in action. On each activity page, you will see a box labelled Watch, listen, reflect. This box contains suggestions of what you might look and listen for as you work and play with young babies. Much of the time you will watch, listen and <u>remember</u>, using your knowledge of early years and of the children to reflect on the progress of the individual child. These informal observations will help you to plan the next day's or week's activities.

However, sometimes, what you see is new evidence - something you have never seen the baby do before, or something which concerns you. In these cases you might make a written note of the achievement or concern you experience, with the date and time you observed it. You can use these notes for a range of different purposes:

- to remind you of the event or achievement (it's easy to forget in a busy setting!)
- to use in discussion with your manager or other practitioners
- to contribute to the child's profile or record
- to discuss with parents
- to help with identifying or supporting additional needs
- to help with planning for individuals and groups
- to make sure you tell everyone about the child's achievements.

Observation is a crucial part of the complex job you do, and time spent observing and listening to children is never wasted.

Your role as practitioner or parent will be varied and will include:

* Facilitating	* Observing	* Prompting	* Negotiating
* Supporting	* Imitating	* Celebrating	* Acknowledging

Watch, Listen and Reflect

Keeping safe

Safety must be the top priority when working with any baby or young child, in your setting or at home. All the activities in Little Baby Books are suitable for under threes. You will already have a health and safety policy but here are just a few tips for safe play with babies and young children.

Watch for choking hazards

Young babies and children naturally explore toys by bringing them to their mouths. This is fine, but always check that toys are clean. If you are concerned, buy a choke measure from a high street baby shop.

Never leave babies or young children unattended

They are naturally inquisitive and this needs to be encouraged, BUT they need you to watch out for them. Make sure you are always there.

Check for sharp edges

Some everyday objects or wooden toys can splinter. Check all toys and equipment regularly. Don't leave this to chance – make a rota.

Ribbons and string

Mobiles and toys tied to baby gyms are great to encourage looking and reaching, but do check regularly that they are fastened securely. Ribbons and string are fascinating for babies and children of all ages – but they can be a choking hazard.

Clean spaces

Babies are natural explorers. They need clean floors. Store outdoor shoes away from the under-threes area.

Sitters and standers

Make sure of a soft landing for babies and young children just getting there with sitting and standing balance. Put a pillow behind babies who are just starting to sit. Keep the area clear of hard objects, such as wooden bricks. Look out for trip hazards for crawlers and walkers.

Make sure babies and young children are fastened securely into high chairs and that chairs are moved out of the way when not in use. Use a low chair and table for young children. Try to make a foot-rest if their feet don't reach the ground. Watch out for chairs that tip easily.

Contents

Contents

Contents

Contents

Aspect and components

Section 1

The Following section contains activities for young children, to help build **a Strong Child**

The relevant Birth to Three Matters components are:
* **Me Myself and I**
* **A Sense of Belonging**
* **Being Acknowledged and Affirmed**
* **Developing Self-assurance**

Movers, shakers and players

Aspect:
A Strong Child

Components:
Me, myself and I
A sense of belonging

14

Making Faces
expressions

What you need

* a book or magazine with people's faces

What you do

1. Sit with one or two children and look at the magazine.
2. When you come to a picture of a face, ask the children how the person is feeling, and how they can tell.
3. Say 'Can you make your face sad (or happy, or cross, or disappointed)?' Keep looking at the picture as the children practise different expressions.
4. Praise their efforts and ask them how they feel when their face is cross, or sad or happy.
5. Try making the faces standing up and making your bodies look cross or sad. Walk around. Then sit down and talk about how you felt.

another idea:
* Read some stories about feelings. The game will help children to empathise with the characters.

Ready for more?

✋ Make a game with pictures cut from magazines and stuck on card. Take turns to turn over a card and make the expression. This will help children to understand their feelings.

Individual needs

- ☼ Try with just one picture.
- ☼ Use an unbreakable mirror so the children can see their expressions.
- ☼ Use expressive puppets or dolls to help children explore feelings. Don't make the experience turn into something negative or destructive.

Tiny Tip

✳ Always finish the game with a happy face.

Watch, listen, reflect

- 👁 Watch and listen to their comments and whether they can discriminate between expressions.
- 👁 With older children, note the words they use to describe feelings, and their ability to empathise with others - feeling with them.
- 👁 Watch to see if they can adopt physical postures - a sad walk, cross stomping.

Working together

Parents could:

- ✳ play the expressions games at home.
- ✳ collect suitable pictures and photos for you to use in feelings games.

Practitioners could:

- ✳ talk openly about feelings, negative as well as positive ones. Admit to being human yourselves!
- ✳ collect suitable stories and picture books to use in discussions.

I like you - you like me

Self awareness, identity

What are they learning?

are they
   exploring
   expressions?
   feeling?
   looking?
   sharing?
   describing?
   moving?
this leads to
   ✳ responding
   ✳ empathising

Self awareness,
identity

**Movers, shakers
and players**

Aspect:
A Strong Child

Components:
Me, myself and I
A sense of belonging

Touch Your Nose
names of features

What you need
* no special equipment

What you do
1. Sit on the floor with the baby (or babies).
2. Put your finger on your nose. Say 'Can you put your finger on your nose?' Praise them if they can.
3. Now put your finger on your ear, your mouth, cheek, hair etc. Name each feature as you touch it, and ask the children to copy you. encourage and praise.
4. Now ask the child to gently touch your nose (or ear, hair, face etc).
5. If the children can follow these instructions, see if they can play the game gently touching each others' features.

another idea:
* Bring a doll to the game and touch her features. Remember to name each feature as you touch it and say 'Here is the doll's hair/eye/ear', or other feature.

Ready for more?
- Look at some pictures of children or adults and talk about their features. Compare hair colour etc. with the child's own.
- Play the game when looking in the mirror.

- Use a small dab of moisturiser to draw attention to your features or the child's.
- Use a puppet to gently touch the child's features, but watch carefully for any signs of anxiety.
- Give them plenty of time to explore your features.

Tiny Tip

* Take some photos of the children and make a picture book.

- Listen for single words and phrases such as 'Mike ear' or 'Susy hair', naming themselves or others.
- Listen, copy and praise any words they use.
- Watch how they touch their own and each other's faces.
- Note when they look and feel features on dolls or pictures when they are playing.

Working together

Parents could:

* bring in family photos for your album.
* help their children to learn the names of features.
* tell practitioners when their children learn new words and phrases.

Practitioners could:

* put safety mirrors low down so children can see themselves as they play on the floor.
* repeat this activity when they are changing or washing children.

I like you – you like me

Self awareness, identity

What are they learning?

are they
  naming?
  recognising their own features?
  having fun?
  looking carefully?
  copying?
this leads to
  * awareness of self
  * comparing

Movers, shakers and players

Aspect:
A Strong Child

Components:
Me, myself and I
A sense of belonging

18

Pat-a-Cake
finger games for two people

What you need
* an unbreakable mirror

What you do
1. Sit with the child in your lap and the mirror propped up close and facing you. Hold the child's hands and play patting games on the mirror. Pat with one hand, then with both. Play clap then pat, both hands then one. Enjoy it!
2. Children often need several sessions of this before playing with a partner.
3. Now sit opposite the child, either on two chairs or cushions, or on the floor. Play the patting and clapping game again, this time with each other. Pat both hands, pat one hand, clap, then pat one hand or both hands. This needs practice and timing!
4. Now try the rhyme, 'Pat a Cake'.

another idea:
* Play patting in shaving foam or finger paint.

Ready for more?
👋 When the children are experienced at patting games with you, try a small group in pairs.
👋 Add slapping on their knees, thighs or legs as another variation.

Individual needs

- ☼ Give them plenty of practice in patting on a flat surface first.
- ☼ Try patting bubbles on a table top.
- ☼ Try putting glove puppets or gloves on your and their hands to draw their attention to what they are doing. Sewing a bell on each glove is fun!

Tiny Tip

❄ Remind children to pat gently on other people's faces!

Watch, listen, reflect

- Watch them in the mirror, are they watching their hands?
- Listen to any words and sounds they say or ones they copy from you.
- Praise them when they join in with the words and rhymes you are saying.
- Note how they are managing clapping and patting with both hands.

Working together

Parents could:

* play finger games and rhymes with their children.
* take turns in simple things like throwing socks into the washing machine, putting toys in a box, turning over the pages of a magazine or book.

Practitioners could:

* make sure there are mirrors at child height so children can practice mirror clapping and patting.
* collect finger and hand rhymes and songs.
* play clapping games outside in the garden.

I like you - you like me

Self awareness, identity

What are they learning?

are they
- watching?
- sharing?
- enjoying?
- sharing?
- feeling?
- responding?

this leads to
- * imitating
- * responding
- * turn taking

Movers, shakers and players

Aspect:
A Strong Child

Components:
Me, myself and I
A sense of belonging

20

After You!
sharing food and eating

What you need
* a child sized tea set, with teapot, cups and cutlery
* some pretend food
* a small table and chairs

What you do
You could try this with one, two or three children. It's about taking turns.
1. Sit on a chair each and play tea parties. Start with the tea set in a bowl or basket.
2. Encourage the children to share out the cups etc, so everyone has one.
3. Help the children to share the party, pouring tea, passing round food, saying 'Please' and 'Thank you'. Model this yourself, and praise them when they do it.
4. Encourage turn taking, use of cutlery etc.

another idea:
* Try this with real food, including cutting up sandwiches or cake, spreading bread and sharing out small sweets or pieces of fruit. Or just try with water in the teapot.

Ready for more?
* Use group times to help children practise passing things, taking turns, saying 'Please' and 'Thank you'.
* Play other simple turn taking games, cards, pairs, snap etc. Limit the group to 2 or 3.

Individual needs

☼ Play pass it to you, pass it back to me with one child.

☼ Play turn taking with a simple toy that moves or plays a noise.

☼ Take turns in taking straws out of a tin, beads out of a cup, putting bricks in a post box, before playing group games.

Tiny Tip

✱ Sometimes have too many things for the group and discuss the left overs.

Watch, listen, reflect

👁 Listen to their conversations and note new words.

👁 Praise their use of 'Please' and 'Thank you'.

👁 Watch how their skills of pouring, cutting, spooning are developing.

👁 Prompt them to take turns and look at others when they speak to them.

Working together

Parents could:

✱ let their children help with preparing and serving meals.

✱ involve the children in turn taking when shopping, playing at the park, even walking, running, jumping.

Practitioners could:

✱ model turn taking and responsive behaviour among adults!

✱ check there are plenty of opportunities to take turns in games and daily group times.

I like you - you like me

Self awareness, identity

What are they learning?

are they
taking turns?
sharing?
talking?
copying?
using 'Please' and 'Thank you'?
this leads to
* listening carefully
* responding

Movers, shakers and players

Aspect:
A Strong Child

Components:
Me, myself and I
A sense of belonging

Mine and Yours
naming, recognising

What you need

* pairs of things - one belonging to them, one not. eg one of their shoes and one of yours; their cup and an adult cup; their hat and a dressing up hat

What you do

1. Put all the things in a pile, and explore them with the child.
2. Now take a pair of objects
3. Hold both objects out to the child and ask 'Which hat is yours?' or 'Which is Marty's hat?'.
4. Encourage the child to look carefully at the two objects and choose the one that is theirs.
5. Praise their efforts in recognising their own things. Say 'Yes, that's your hat. This is my hat.'
6. Play again with two more things.

another idea:
* Play with two children and have things belonging to each.

Ready for more?

☝ Try with a larger group and have a pile of hats or coats and see how quickly they can find their own.
☝ Have objects belonging to babies, adults and the children.

- ☼ Just have one pair of things - eg two hats. Offer both to the child and see if they can choose their own. Praise effort and put the hats on both of you!
- ☼ Talk about ownership each time they get dressed - 'We are putting on Jay's coat, it's your coat isn't it Jay?'

Tiny Tip
- ✳ Charity shops are good places to find items for this activity.

- 👁 Note their recognition of their own belongings.
- 👁 Listen and note any naming and use of 'mine'.
- 👁 Reflect on whether the children are encouraged to be independent in finding their own things.
- 👁 Watch children as they find and use things, recognising their own and others' belongings.

Working together

Parents could:
- ✳ encourage their children to fetch and put on their own coats, shoes and other belongings.
- ✳ give children their own space at home to keep their own things, even their own plate and cup. This gives them an awareness of self.

Practitioners could:
- ✳ arrange for children to have and recognise their own things - cups, pegs, clothing etc.
- ✳ explain to parents why this is an important skill for young children and helps them to develop independence.

I like you - you like me

Self awareness, identity

What are they learning?

are they
   recognising?
   naming?
   selecting?
   looking carefully?
   responding?
this leads to
   * self awareness
   * independence

Movers, shakers and players

Aspect:
A Strong Child

Components:
Me, myself and I
Being acknowledged & affirmed

24

Scrunchy Fun
arms and legs, fingers and toes

What you need

* bracelets, hair scrunchies
* lengths of ribbon and interesting fabric
* a basket

What you do

1. Tie lengths of ribbon and strips of fabric to make bracelets that go easily around an arm. Put these and the bracelets and hair scrunchies in the box.
2. Sit on the floor with two or perhaps three children. Pass the box around for each child to feel. Tip the box out onto the floor and spend some time exploring the contents, choosing favourites and trying them on.
3. Make sure each child has several bracelets on each arm, and then sing together, to the tune of 'Here we go Round the Mulberry Bush':

   'This is the way we shake our hands, shake our hands, shake our hands
   This is the way we shake our hands, shake, shake, shake'.
4. Next help the children to put the bracelets on their ankles.
5. Lie down together in the circle and shake your feet!

Ready for more?

- Spread the bangles and bracelets on the floor. Dance around and when the music stops, each choose one to put on.
- Pass a bangle round the circle, each child putting it on the child next to them.

Individual needs

✿ Make sure the bracelets are easy enough for all the children to manage.

✿ For less mobile children, play the game at a table.

✿ Sew bells to strips of brightly coloured ribbons to play this game with a visually impaired child.

Tiny Tip

❋ Young children will often spontaneously fill a gap in a song, even if they haven't been singing along!

Watch, listen, reflect

👁 Watch the way children explore the contents of the box and make their choices.

👁 Observe how children use gesture to support their first words. Look at the way they use language to communicate with each other, and with you.

👁 Listen for first words and two word phrases.

Working together

Parents could:

* play passing back and forth games at home. Why not have a tiny tug of war with socks at bedtime?

* play at balancing bath toys on their child's knees, arms, hands at bath time.

Practitioners could:

* put a list of items they need for this activity on the parents notice board.

* fix a note for parents, next to the dressing up clothes and mirror, about the importance of dressing up play and suggesting some ideas to try at home.

Look at me

Finding an identity

What are they learning?

are they
   playing together?
   taking turns?
   making choices?
   saying rhymes?

this leads to
   * co-operating
   * being part of a group
   * joining in

Look at Me

Finding an identity

Movers, shakers and players

Aspect:
A Strong Child

Components:
Me, myself and I
Being acknowledged & affirmed

26

So Big!
looking at shapes and sizes

What you need

* full length mirror at child height
* big shoes, huge wellies, enormous fluffy slippers
* tiny baby shoes and socks
* extra large gloves and tiny baby mittens

What you do

1. Spread out all the shoes, socks and gloves on the floor. Sit with the children as they explore them.
2. Talk about the size of the items. Try some on. Encourage two word phrases, such as 'big boots', or 'too small'.
3. Look in the mirror and talk with the children about what you see, such as 'big gloves' and 'little hands'.
4. Put hands and feet next to the shoes and gloves and compare sizes.
5. Put your hands and feet next to the children's!

another idea:
* See how high up the mirror you can reach. Add stickers and pictures to mark each child's reach.

Ready for more?

* Look at pictures and photos of babies. Look how small their hands and feet are.
* Take some digital photos of the children in the shoes and boots. Match the pictures to the real objects and people.

Individual needs

☼ For children at an early developmental stage, stick a photo of them as they are now, next to the mirror. Keep showing them their reflection, pointing to the photo and saying 'Look, it's *name*. I can see you!' giving them a gentle tickle and smile.

☼ Spend lots of time looking at photos.

Tiny Tip

✳ Why not cover role play boxes and label with a photo or picture of the contents.

Watch, listen, reflect

👁 Watch how children make connections between what they do and what they see in the mirror

👁 Listen for describing words and two word phrases.

👁 Think about how the children are using each other's ideas to develop their own play.

Working together

Parents could:

* put a mirror up at home at the right height for their child to be able to see their reflection.
* fill an old suitcase or box with old clothes and accessories for dressing up play.

Practitioners could:

* review the 'dressing up play' provided. Look at how this can be extended and improved. Include parents and children in your plans.
* make sure there are easily accessible mirrors in different parts of your setting.

What are they learning?

are they
   exploring?
   copying?
   looking?
   recognising themselves?
   smiling?

this leads to
   * concentrating
   * matching

Movers, shakers and players

Aspect:
A Strong Child

Components:
Me, myself and I
Being acknowledged & affirmed

Bath Time Dolly!
looking at bodies

What you need

* a doll for each child
* bowl of soapy water, flannel, sponge and brush
* towel
* small plastic beaker or jug

What you do

1. Spend some time bathing the doll. Check that the child understands simple body part words. As they play, ask them to, wash dolly's knees, or perhaps clean dolly's ears. See if they can show you their knees and ears too.
2. Using the jug, trickle water onto dolly as you sing, using a tune you are comfortable with,
   'Water on my tummy, water on my toes
   Water on my fingers, and even on my nose'.
3. Then, give the child the flannel and sing *'Flannel on my tummy, flannel on my toes ...'*, encouraging them to wash dolly with the flannel.

another idea:
* Bathe toy animals, practising body part words as you go.

Ready for more?

🖐 Look at picture books about babies. Talk about body parts. Compare the babies' hands and feet with the children's.
🖐 Make a book of baby photos and pictures of baby clothes, cots, bottles and so on.

Individual needs

☼ Use a dry or barely damp flannel to wash their hands and your hands and faces. Focus on learning just one or two body part words.

☼ Work in a good light with children with visual impairment, washing the doll with a brightly coloured damp flannel. Give them plenty of time to explore the doll.

Tiny Tip

✳ try to get some of the tiny soaps and shampoo bottles left as a courtesy in hotel bathrooms.

Watch, listen, reflect

👁 Watch to see if the children understand the body part words. Look for them understanding the body part words on their own bodies, too.

👁 Listen for first words, phrases, natural gesture and pointing.

👁 Think about what they understand about growing, and the different needs of babies and children.

Working together

Parents could:

★ bring in baby photos.
★ give their child a doll to wash as part of their own bath time play, joining in with this simple pretend play.
★ show their child their baby photos and things that they did when he/she was a tiny baby.

Practitioners could:

★ add baby care items (eg. doll's highchair & baby bath) to the home corner.
★ put up baby photos and add catalogues of baby care equipment.
★ invite parents to bring new babies into nursery to spend some time with the children.

Look at me

Finding an identity

What are they learning?

are they
   using names of body parts?
   talking about growing?
   pretending?
   caring?

this leads to
   ★ exploring change
   ★ differences

Movers, shakers and players

Aspect:
A Strong Child

Components:
Me, myself and I
Being acknowledged & affirmed

30

Dip Those Toes
exploring new textures

What you need

* four plastic trays or washing up bowls
* warm soapy water
* cold, wet sand
* tiny pebbles
* fur fabric

What you do

1. Cover the bottom of the first plastic tray with a few centimetres of warm soapy water. Put a thin layer of cold sand in the second, and a layer of pebbles in the third. Cover the base of the last tray with the fur fabric.
2. Sit with the children and pull off your socks. Play a game of 'Everybody do this, everybody do this, just like me', wiggling toes, pointing toes in the air, walking on heels, etc.
3. Feel the cool of the floor, the roughness of the carpet, etc.
4. With each child sitting on a small chair, together dip your toes gently in the first tray. Talk about how it feels, such as 'Tom is splashing, Kirsty is wiggling her toes.'
5. Swap trays, playing together in each in turn. Encourage the children to use just their toes. Finish with a dip in clean warm water, tickling toes as you dry them.

Ready for more?

🖐 Try trays of bark, compost, cold cooked spaghetti.
🖐 Try making footprints on black paper with water.
🖐 Put a soapy mixture on a tray or tin lid. Draw patterns with your toes.

Individual needs

☼ Some children may be reluctant to give this a try. Why not give them a doll and dip the doll's toes in? 'I wonder if dolly likes it?'

☼ Some children with physical difficulties may have very sensitive feet. Check this out with parents first.

Tiny Tip

✸ Check for allergies and allow plenty of time for washing and drying each child's feet.

Watch, listen, reflect

👁 Watch to see children's reactions. How are they communicating their ideas?

👁 Listen to see if the children are relating this to their own experiences, such as 'This is like our yard', and so on.

👁 Watch to see if they understand that different people may have different likes and dislikes.

Working together

Parents could:

* play at stamping in puddles together.
* try the 'This little piggy went to market' toe rhyme when drying toes.

Practitioners could:

* look at developing the range of sensory play experiences they offer.
* try this activity in the garden of their setting.

Look at me

Finding an identity

What are they learning?

are they
   playing together?
   trying things?
   feeling?
   talking?
   naming?
   imagining?
   taking turns?
this leads to
   * investigating
   * describing

31

Movers, shakers and players

Aspect:
A Strong Child

Components:
Me, myself and I
Being acknowledged & affirmed

32

Shiver and Shake
taking the lead

What you need

* large sheets of crinkly paper
* long lengths of ribbon

What you do

1. Give the children the lengths of ribbon. Play at shaking them, twirling them, swinging them up and down. See how fast they can run with them, blowing in the air. Comment on what the children are doing.
2. Choose one child's action, show it to all the children and see if they can copy it. Try to imitate the children, commenting positively on the way they are using the ribbons.
3. Let them take the lead. Do the same with crinkly paper.
4. Next use the two together. Trail the ribbons on and under the paper, wriggling and jiggling it. Comment and copy the children's actions. Try *'Everybody do this, do this, do this, everybody do this, just like me.'*

another idea:
* Give them a large blanket. Watch what they do with it!

Ready for more?

👋 Sit in a circle and using just one shaker, pass it round the circle, each child in turn copying your first action.

👋 Take shoes off and lie on the floor together, all in a row. Now try all rolling over in turn!

Individual needs

☼ Play alongside children who need encouragement. Allow plenty of time for them to watch you and other children.

☼ Give children plenty of time and space to try out their own ideas.

☼ Look for bright yellow tape and fluorescent coloured ribbons for visually impaired children.

Tiny Tip

✻ A simple thumbs up or wink is a great way to acknowledge the efforts of children who feel shy or less confident.

Watch, listen, reflect

👁 Observe how children try out new ideas and extend ideas that they see and are imitating.

👁 Think about how the children respond to different kinds of praise and encouragement.

👁 Listen for describing words and two and three word phrases.

Working together

Parents could:

* save suitable ribbons and paper for this activity.

* practice watching their child's play and joining in by imitating and playing alongside, rather than directing the activity.

Practitioners could:

* talk to parents about different ways to join in play.

* look at all the different ways praise and positive encouragement are used in their setting, and talk about how to extend and develop this further.

Look at me

Finding an identity

What are they learning?

are they
looking?
imitating?
taking turns?
sharing fun?
trying ideas?

this leads to
* self esteem
* relationships
* being in a group

Confidence and
competence

Movers, shakers
and players

Aspect:
A Strong Child

Components:
Developing self
assurance

34

Put it In, Put it On
posting and stacking

What you need

* make a simple posting toy from
  a small box - you could make a
  hole on the top of the box and
  use bricks, cotton reels, coins,
  socks, Duplo bricks or other
  objects to post

What you do

You can play this game with one or two children. Even a simple,
one-hole box gives young children a real sense of success.

1. Sit opposite the children with the posting toy between
   you and all the posting shapes on the floor.
2. Show the children how to post the objects in the hole.
3. Now offer one of the babies an object and encourage
   them to post it in the hole. Give them plenty of praise
   for efforts and success.
4. Take turns to post objects in the box until they are all
   gone. Say 'All gone!' and 'More?'.
5. If they want to play again, tip the objects out and start
   again.

another idea:

* Make additional holes in the box, or make a smaller hole.

Ready for more?

- Play a game with a
  stacking toy, taking
  turns to put a ring on
  or to balance a beaker.
- Try a simple Feely Bag
  or box, and play taking
  things out of the bag
  and putting them back
  in again.

Individual needs

- ☼ Make a small box with a big posting hole. Cover it with shiny paper to attract the child's attention.
- ☼ Put a metal tin lid in the bottom of the box so the objects make a noise as you take turns to post them in.

Tiny Tip

❋ Collect boxes of all shapes and sizes for posting toys, and hair scrunchies to thread on a post for a bargain toy.

Watch, listen, reflect

- 👁 Look for emerging concepts of taking turns.
- 👁 Watch how they use their hands and fingers to grasp and release the objects into the boxes.
- 👁 Listen for words such as 'All gone'.
- 👁 Watch for signs of enjoyment and achievement, and developing concentration.

Working together

Parents could:

- ✱ make a simple posting box at home from a cereal packet or small box.
- ✱ practice turn taking by passing toys to each other, and passing a spoon between them at mealtime.

Practitioners could:

- ✱ put some posting and threading toys in the Toy Library.
- ✱ watch individual children for emerging schemas of posting, wrapping, filling and emptying. Share observations with parents.

I can do it

Confidence and competence

What are they learning?

are they
taking turns?
holding and
releasing?
enjoying success?
this leads to
* co-operating
* self esteem
* playing games

**Movers, shakers
and players**

In You Go!
tunnels and tents

What you need

* a play tunnel or a drape over
  some chairs to make a tunnel
* a pop up tent or home made
  fabric tent

What you do

This game is very popular for groups of two or three children,
and gives them a real sense of achievement.

1. Let the children watch and help you put up the tunnel
   and/or tent. Talk to them about what you are doing.
2. Sit near the entrance to the tunnel and encourage the
   children to take turns going through the tunnel.
3. If they are cautious or anxious, put a soft toy at the end
   of the tunnel, or make it shorter.
4. Praise the children as they emerge from the other end of
   the tunnel. Remember that for some children, this is a real
   test of bravery and endurance!

another idea:
* Go through the tunnel yourself and get them to clap you
  for your bravery!

Aspect:
A Strong Child

Components:
Developing self
assurance

36

Ready for more?

* Make the tunnel longer
  or put the pop up tent
  at the end for them to
  crawl into.
* Make a junior obstacle
  race outside with
  tunnels, small steps,
  tents and other things
  to climb.

Individual needs

○ Children with restricted movement will love going through a tunnel with you!
○ Hang some ribbons or bells from a sheet of fabric and hold it over their head to make a roof.
○ Use net or transparent fabric for anxious children, so they can see out.

Tiny Tip

✳ Try seaside shops for cheap tents and tunnels. Or use a parachute or big piece of fabric.

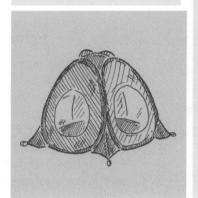

Watch, listen, reflect

👁 Watch the way children explore the tunnels and tents.
👁 Look at levels of confidence and fear. Note particular difficulties, such as going in, or bends in tunnels.
👁 Listen and watch for expressions and sounds of success. Be vigilant for children who are frightened of being enclosed.

Working together

Parents could:

* help their children make dens and tents at home.
* have fun under the bed-clothes when they get up, or when they make the beds.

Practitioners could:

* put photos of simple home made tents and dens on the parents' notice board.
* talk with parents about fears and excitement in their own children, and the importance of helping children to overcome their fears.

Confidence and competence

What are they learning?
are they
   taking safe risks?
   enjoying it?
   experiencing success?
   playing together?
this leads to
   * co-operating
   * self esteem
   * overcoming fears

37

Confidence and
competence

Movers, shakers
and players

Aspect:
A Strong Child

Components:
A sense of belonging

Up and Down
stairs, steps, slides

What you need

* a small set of children's steps
  (as in picture) OR
* some safe steps or stairs
  indoors or outside

What you do

Climbing up and down steps and stairs needs plenty of
practice and praise. Play this game with one or two children.
1. Start at the bottom of the steps.
2. Hold the children's hands and climb the steps with them.
   Say or sing *'Up we go, up we go, one two, up we go'*.
3. When you get to the top, say *'Well done, we climbed up.
   What can we see from up at the top?'*
4. Turn round and step down the steps, singing *'Down we go,
   down we go, one two, down we go'*.
5. Go slowly, so the children have time to put both feet on
   each step if they need to.
6. Repeat this song and movement several times.

another idea:

* Practice singing and walking up the steps of a low slide.

Ready for more?

✋ Put heavy bricks or
blocks (or two sets of
play steps) together to
make an 'up and down'
staircase.

✋ Make some little steps
with bricks for teddies
and dolls to go up and
down.

Individual needs

☼ Make sure there are rails beside steps in your setting and garden.

☼ Give children plenty of time and praise for this difficult skill.

☼ Remember, going up is much easier than going down!

Safety Tip!

❄ Babies and young children should never be left unattended near stairs until they can manage going up AND down safely.

Watch, listen, reflect

👁 Note how soon children can climb steps on their own. Look at how they climb - one foot, both feet, one foot, both feet, or one foot at a time up the steps.

👁 Remember that children learn better if they have plenty of praise. Observe yourself and other practitioners to make sure you give plenty of feedback.

Working together

Parents could:

★ give their child plenty of opportunity to climb steps with help and independently.

★ let children walk along low walls and steps when they are out on walks.

Practitioners could:

★ make sure steps and stairs are safely used, and protected with stair gates when adults are not around.

★ help parents to understand safe ways of learning about steps and stairs.

I can do it

Trust, confidence and self worth

What are they learning?

are they
   climbing?
   practicing?
   experiencing success?
   being praised?
this leads to
   * self esteem
   * confidence
   * self assurance

Movers, shakers and players

Aspect:
A Strong Child

Components:
Developing self assurance

40

Snip, Snap!
cutting and snipping

What you need

* safe scissors
* plenty of paper - eg magazine pages, recycled paper, junk mail, wallpaper, wrapping paper, envelopes

What you do

This activity is about confidence and self assurance in cutting - not 'cutting out'. A small group would enjoy it.

1. Cut some of the paper into long thin strips, so that the children can snip across them in one cut.
2. Leave some of the paper in bigger pieces.
3. Sit at a table with the children, and talk about cutting and snipping as they work. Give plenty of encouragement.
4. Help children if they need it, by holding the paper as they snip, or by putting your hand over theirs on the scissors.
5. Help them to snip the long pieces into bits, or snip round the edges of bigger pieces.

another idea:
* Snip the edges of pieces of coloured paper and use them as place mats for snack time.

Ready for more?

* Sometimes, let them fringe the edges of their drawings or paintings.
* Snip lengths of coloured or shiny paper and stick them on a strip of card for an individual crown.

- ✿ Search out some specialised scissors for children with poor grip, and for left handers.
- ✿ Sit facing the child and hold the paper so they can snip from their side.
- ✿ Sometimes let the child hold the paper as you snip.

Tiny Tip

❋ Scissors must be sharp enough to cut, or children will get frustrated and discouraged.

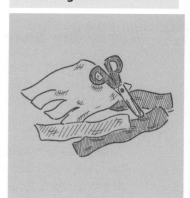

- 👁 Watch the way children hold the scissors and give plenty of encouragement and modelling to help them improve.
- 👁 Listen to them talk as they cut - you will get some interesting observations!
- 👁 Note how well they concentrate on learning and practising this difficult skill.

Working together

Parents could:

- ★ let their children practice with suitable scissors at home.
- ★ be patient when children just snip and snip!

Practitioners could:

- ★ advise parents about suitable scissors for their children.
- ★ make sure children have plenty of safe practice with snipping at the early stage of learning scissor skills.

I can do it

Trust, confidence and self worth

What are they learning?

are they
   concentrating?
   experiencing
   success?
   using both hands?
This leads to
   * self assurance
   * fine motor
     skills
   * confidence

I can do It

Confidence and competence

Movers, shakers and players

Aspect:
A Strong Child

Components:
Developing self assurance

42

Peg It!
pegboard play

What you need

* wooden or plastic peg boards with holes
* different coloured pegs in small bowls

What you do

This activity supports fine motor control and a sense of achievement. Three or four children could play together.

1. Sit with the children at a table.
2. Talk about the pegs and peg boards and model how they are used.
3. Play alongside the children, making patterns, putting the pegs in and taking them out. Talk about what you are doing as you work.
4. Look at the children's work too, giving praise and encouragement. Looking at each other's patterns, talking about colours and shapes.

another idea:
* Try making a one-line pattern for them to copy. Then get them to make one for you to copy.

Ready for more?

🖐 Roll out a big piece of dough and use it as a group peg board. When it is full of holes, roll it out again.
🖐 Take turns with one or two children to put a peg in a board. You could have a colour each.

Individual needs

- ☼ Make sure the pegs are easy to put in and get out.
- ☼ Look for big pegs and boards with bigger holes.
- ☼ Stick the board down to the table with blutack to steady it for children with poor motor control.

Tiny Tip

✳ Float the pegs in a bowl of bubbly water to make a different sort of game!

Watch, listen, reflect

- 👁 Watch to see if the children can follow the simple routine and rules of this game.
- 👁 Listen to how the children negotiate with each other. Listen for short phrases where they predict what might happen next.
- 👁 Look for developing finger/thumb control.

Working together

Parents could:

- * chop up some straws into short lengths and make a game of pushing them into flour and water, pastry or wet sand.
- * try clipping clothes pegs onto a low level washing line.

Practitioners could:

- * put some pegs and boards in the toy library or loan collection.
- * provide some 'take home' dough or a recipe for it.

I can do it

Trust, confidence and self worth

What are they learning?

are they
   concentrating?
   using fingers and
   hands?
   having fun?
   making patterns?
this leads to
   * concentration
   * self assurance
   * fine motor
      skills

Me and my world

Trust, confidence and self worth

Movers, shakers and players

Aspect:
A Strong Child

Components:
A sense of belonging

44

Rocking and Watching
a rocker snuggle song

What you need

* a blanket or piece of soft fabric
* a cushion
* a soft toy

What you do

1. Sit opposite the child, with the child on the cushion, holding the soft toy. Put the blanket gently around the child's shoulders.
2. Grip the blanket firmly at each edge and practise rocking side to side. Rock the child gently too.
3. As you rock together from side to side, with the child wrapped in the blanket opposite you, sing:

    Rocking, rocking, side to side
    Teddy bear all snug and warm
    Hugging me and hugging you
    Rocking, rocking, side to side.

another idea:
* Play with two children. Give them a teddy each, wrapped in a blanket to rock from side to side, as you sing.

Ready for more?

* Make a small hammock for soft toys with a blanket. Sing 'Rock a Bye Baby' and other songs with the children.
* Snuggle all together under a big blanket and sing 'Ten in a Bed' and other songs.

Individual needs

- ☼ Some children find rocking a huge comfort or very rewarding. Consider why the child is rocking so much.
- ☼ This simple pretend play, imitating actions - hugging or putting to bed - is good for children on the autistic spectrum.
- ☼ Make sure children with physical or sensory difficulties feel safe.

Tiny Tip

✳ Give children a cushion to sit on at group times. It reminds them of what they need to do and where they need to sit!!

Watch, listen, reflect

- 👁 Look to see if the child is anticipating the actions of the song.
- 👁 Watch to see if they carry on the 'caring for teddy' pretend play after the song.
- 👁 Listen for first words and attempts to join in with the song.
- 👁 Are the children passively letting you rock them in the blanket, or can they sway from side to side.

Working together

Parents could:

- ✳ rock, sway and dance with their child.
- ✳ encourage simple pretend play such as feeding dolls and so on.

Practitioners could:

- ✳ talk to parents about the importance of simple pretend play and home corner play to their child's emerging understanding of familiar situations and their feelings.
- ✳ share examples of when their child has been offered and made choices.

Me and my world

Trust, confidence and self worth

What are they learning?

are they
   trusting?
   confident?
   balancing?
   imitating?
   showing care?
this leads to
- * self assurance
- * confidence
- * pretend play
- * being in a group

Trust, confidence and self worth

Movers, shakers and players

Aspect:
A Strong Child

Components:
A sense of belonging

Terrific Trains
a gentle cha-cha

What you need

* a big space, preferably a carpeted area
* some suitable music with a strong beat or a cha-cha

What you do

This game is very popular! Play it with a small group.

1. Sit with the children one behind another and help them to stretch their hands out in front so that they are resting their hands on the shoulders of the child in front.
2. Talk about gentle touches and no tugs!! Practise resting hands on and then taking them off when the music stops.
3. Now stand up together and put hands on shoulders and set the music off. Lead the children one behind the other, moving slowly to the music. Stop the music often. When the music stops, put hands down!
4. Have lots of fun with this cha-cha, focusing on stopping when the music stops and being gentle with other children.

another idea:

* Find some marching music, and march along a chalked line.

Ready for more?

🖐 Hold a bunch of ties or ribbons. With a child holding the end of each ribbon, dance in a ring. Stop and start to music

🖐 Try moving together with a partner, or dancing under an arch made with the raised arms of two children.

Individual needs

☼ Practise dancing the cha-cha with just one other child for children with less confidence or more mature children.

☼ Lead facing children with autistic spectrum disorders. You will need to move backwards!!

☼ Use a flag or light to signal that the music has stopped.

Tiny Tip

❋ Getting down to child's eye-level is one of the most effective strategies for helping them to listen and attend to what you are saying.

Watch, listen, reflect

👁 Look to see if the children are showing an emerging awareness of the needs of the other children.

👁 Are they able to move confidently alongside other children?

👁 Listen to the range of ways the children are using first words and short phrases to talk to each other.

👁 Think about the ways children are offered and respond to praise.

Working together

Parents could:

* play 'Follow my Leader' and other traditional games with their child.
* step and jump alongside their child, copying and taking turns with simple actions.

Practitioners could:

* try making trains with children moving one behind another as a way to move from one area of the setting to another.
* talk about the way children are encouraged to express their own needs and to show an awareness of others' needs.

Me and my world

Trust, confidence and self worth

What are they learning?

are they
    showing care and
    concern?
    expressing own
    needs?
this leads to
    * confidence
    * awareness of
      own needs and
      needs of others
    * sense of belonging

Movers, shakers and players

Aspect:
A Strong Child

Components:
A sense of belonging

48

Bouncy, Bouncy
trampoline fun

What you need

* a small trampoline, a space hopper or exercise ball

What you do

1. Help the child to climb onto the trampoline. Stand facing them, holding their hands and gently bounce them up and down to get the feel of the springs. If you are using a hopper or ball, help the child to lie over it on their tummy.
2. Hold them carefully by their sides. Bounce them very gently so they get the feel of the springy motion.
3. Standing so that the child can easily gaze into your eyes, chant briskly, bouncing the child gently up and down to the rhythm of the chant:

Ready .... And

Up, down, up, down, One, two, three,
Up, down, up, down, One, two, three.

(Pause the bouncing, wait for eye contact and shout together)

BOO!

Ready for more?

* Jump together and count to three, chant 'One, two, three, BOO!'
* Use a large beach ball. Stand with 2 children, bouncing the ball up and down. Chant 'Up, down, up, down, stop!'
* Take turns to bounce over soft play shapes.

Individual needs

☼ Try bouncing children with physical difficulties very gently up and down in a strong blanket held by two adults.

☼ Encourage less confident children to get the feel of the bounce by tapping or patting the surface of the trampoline.

☼ This is a great activity for encouraging eye contact.

Safety Tip!

✳ Help children overcome wobbles when standing on uneven surfaces by holding them gently steady at the hips, rather than by the hands.

Watch, listen, reflect

👁 Watch how the child develops confidence as the activity becomes more familiar. Are they able to manage any uncertainty?

👁 Is there a sense of shared fun? How is the child expressing their feelings about the activity?

👁 Listen for first words and phrases, and attempts to join in with key phrases in the rhyme.

Working together

Parents could:

✳ tell practitioners about their child's favourite active play.

✳ sing to their child as they walk and play together, describing actions, such as 'Jumping, jumping, just like me'.

Practitioners could:

✳ encourage parents to help their child have a go at this activity when they collect them at the end of a session.

✳ talk about the range of physical play opportunities for young children in their area.

Me and my world

Trust, confidence and self worth

What are they learning?

are they
    sharing fun?
    expressing feelings?
    developing confidence?
this leads to
    * trust
    * confidence
    * self esteem

Trust, confidence and self worth

Movers, shakers and players

Aspect:
A Strong Child

Components:
A sense of belonging

Look at Me, Can You See?
finding out about body parts

What you need

* space for a circle of children on a carpeted area

What you do

1. Sit on the floor with the children, legs stretched out in front and hands on knees.
2. Ask the children to join in with the actions, chant gradually getting quicker and quicker, until you chant the last line very slowly.

You can chant these words or make up your own:

Look at me, can you see
Can you see, can you see?
Hands-a-shaking, hands-a-shaking
Fingers tapping, fingers tapping
Elbows touching, elbows touching
Hands on knees.

Make the next chant about legs and feet:

Look at me, can you see
Can you see, can you see?
Feet-a-stamping, feet-a-stamping
Legs-a-bending, legs-a-bending
Toes-a-wiggling, toes-a-wiggling
Hands on knees.

3. Make up some more 'body chants'.

Ready for more?

- Play 'Here we go Round the Mulberry Bush' with actions linked to a routine, such as dressing, washing or bedtime.
- Pass simple actions around a small circle, such as patting hands, touching noses, touching toes.

50

Individual needs

☼ Try giving each child a cushion to sit on to help with focus and attention.

☼ Play one to one with children with communication difficulties, or autistic spectrum disorders.

☼ Ask a helper to sit behind children who need extra help and do the actions on the child together.

Tiny Tip

❋ Sing hello to each child by name at the beginning of the activity. Make this quick and animated. It helps all children feel an important part of the game.

Watch, listen, reflect

👁 Watch to see if the children are imitating the actions and able to follow the changes of actions.

👁 Listen for the children joining in and anticipating the end of the rhyme.

👁 Are the children able to maintain their attention as part of a group.

👁 Look to see how the children are relating to each other.

Working together

Parents could:

✷ visit the library for books and tapes of action rhymes and songs.

✷ play 'Heads, Shoulders, Knees and Toes' with their child.

Practitioners could:

✷ play a simple circle game with just three children every day. Talk to parents about their child's growing confidence.

✷ make sure every child has a photo with their name and handprint displayed at child level.

Me and my world

Trust, confidence and self worth

What are they learning?

are they
  learning body
  part words?
  imitating actions?
  attending?
  sharing fun?
This leads to
  ✷ listening
  ✷ turn taking
  ✷ being part of a group

Resources for all stages of A Strong Child

Puppets

Make simple puppets from:
* old socks
* jumper sleeves
* gloves
* paper plates

Puppets, persona dolls & soft toys

Puppets by Post

www.puppetsbypost.com

Percussion instruments
* IKEA   * ELC
* Mothercare

For cooking & making food (real & pretend)

* plastic plates and beakers (IKEA)
* small plastic jugs
* spoons with chunky handles for serving
* small knives or butter knives for cutting fruit, bread
* plastic or fabric tablecloths

Phones

Use old mobile phones (with batteries removed) or ask phone shops for out of date demonstration models.

Bubbles

Try shaving foam for really good bubbles and for table top fun. Add ready mixed paint for a new experience.

A good value, easy to use desktop digital printer

Hewlett Packard
HP Photosmart 230

Tents and tunnels

Get pop up tents from beach shops

Heuristic Play

More about heuristic play in 'People Under Three' by Elinor Goldschmied and Sonia Jackson

Baskets, containers, weaving materials, dolly pegs

Mindstretchers
Tel: 07768 882537

Scissors for left handers and children with poor grip

ASCO Suppliers
Tel: 0113 2707070

Post boxes, stacking rings, bean bags, threading toys and peg boards, rolling toys, simple instruments and musical rollers from

ASCO Suppliers
Tel: 0113 2707070

Songs for babies

Rock a Bye Baby
Ride a Cock Horse
Row, Row, Row the Boat
Dance to Your Daddy
Bye Baby Bunting
Hush Little Baby Don't you Cry
Down Among the Fishes in the Deep Blue Sea

Some Finger songs and rhymes

This Little Pig Went to Market
Pat-a-Cake, Pat-a-Cake
Round and Round the Garden
She Didn't Dance
Incy Wincy Spider
Tommy Thumb
Five Little Peas
Two Little Dicky Birds
Wind the Bobbin
My Little House
Here are the Lady's Knives & Forks
Here is a Box
One Potato, Two Potato
Peter Hammers with One Hammer
One Finger, One Thumb Keep Moving
Heads, Shoulders, Knees and Toes
Roly, Poly up and Down
Teddy Bear, Teddy Bear

Dressing up

Try Charity shops and bargain shops for dressing up clothes, hats, domestic objects.

Cheap clothing

Use fabric remnants and scarves for easy dressing up - fasten them with clothes pegs.

Movers, Shakers and Players

Aspect and components

54

Section 2

The Following section contains activities for young children, to help build **a Skilful Communicator**

The relevant Birth to Three Matters components are:
* **Being Together**
* **Finding a Voice**
* **Listening and Responding**
* **Making Meaning**

Aspect and components

Movers, shakers
and players

Aspect:
A Skilful
Communicator

Components:
Being together
Communicating
Finding a voice

What Can It Be?
object words and use

What you need

* 6 everyday objects round a
  theme (eg 6 items of clothing,
  6 items of food, 6 things
  from the bathroom)
* a small bag, basket or
  pillowcase

What you do

1. Give the child the objects to explore. Talk about the
   object, label it. Say 'Surjit, look, shoe'. Show the object's
   use, such as putting it on the child's foot and walking or
   stamping the floor.
2. Allow plenty of time to explore each object. For children
   who attempt to label the object, smile and say, 'Yes, ball'
   or whatever. If children name the object clearly, praise
   reply with an object and action word together, such as
   'Yes, look, teddy's jumping'.
3. Enjoy playing with the objects together.

another idea:
* Play again with groups of vehicles or perhaps kitchen
  stuff, such as pots, spoons, jug and so on.

Ready for more?

✋ Play this game with
groups of pictures of
objects around similar
themes.

✋ Match objects to
pictures, or pictures
to pictures.

Individual needs

✿ For children with special interests, try including some objects or pictures related to their particular interest in the group.

✿ Try photographs of objects for children needing much practise matching objects to pictures

Tiny Tip

✳ Whispering can be a great way to catch the attention of young children.

Watch, listen, reflect

👁 Listen to first words and short phrases. Are they two object words together, an object and action word together, or a describing word and an object word?

👁 Listen out for two word phrases, including possession, such as 'Dad's hat'.

👁 Watch to see how many of the objects and uses are familiar.

Working together

Parents could:

★ listen out for first words and short phrases and share these with staff.

★ extend their child's first words, such as if the child says 'Car', reply with 'Yes, Mummy's car'.

Practitioners could:

★ make sure they are in the habit of using the child's name first, to gain attention, when talking to young children.

★ spend a few minutes each day listening to and talking with each child about something that has caught their attention.

What I really want

Looking, pointing, using sounds & words

What are they learning?

are they
    using objects?
    using first words?
    understanding
    2 word phrases?
    being together?
this leads to
    * commenting
    * making requests
    * understanding

Looking, pointing,
using sounds & words

**Movers, shakers
and players**

Aspect:
A Skilful
Communicator

Components:
Being together
Communicating
Finding a voice

58

It's Mine!
using possessing words

What you need

* ★ washing line at child height
* ★ push on wooden clothes pegs
* ★ baby and adult clothes
* ★ box with baby and adult shoes, mittens, hats
* ★ a nappy, baby's bottle, keys, purse

What you do

1. Help the children to peg the washing on the line. Play alongside them using short phrases, such as 'Daddy's socks', 'Baby's socks' and so on.
2. Help them to explore the box of objects.
3. Use actions and single words and encourage the children to copy and imitate actions.
4. Use single words and two word phrases to label the objects, including possessive words, like 'Baby's bottle', OR 'Mummy's keys'.

another idea:
* Add some pretend food items, for the baby and adults, together with a baby's spoon and cup.

Ready for more?

- 👋 Play at bathing Dolly, focusing on body parts. Such as 'Let's wash Dolly's feet'.
- 👋 Wash outdoor toys. Work on two word phrases, such as 'Let's wash the bike's wheels'

Individual needs

- ☼ Continue to use pointing and natural gesture for as long as needed.
- ☼ Do lots of action rhymes and turn taking games, on a one to one basis to start with.
- ☼ Use a bright yellow washing line against a black background for children with visual difficulties.

Safety Tip

❄ Be careful with washing lines at child height. Make sure both children and staff are aware of the dangers.

Watch, listen, reflect

- 👁 Listen for the different types of short phrases uses, such as object and action words, or object and describing words.
- 👁 Think about the way children are using language, making requests, commenting, reporting earlier events and so on.
- 👁 Watch to see if the children are listening to each other!

Working together

Parents could:

- ✳ use short phrases with object and possession words as part of getting dressed, such as 'Mummy's coat', 'Karen's shoes', and so on.
- ✳ visit the library for some new action rhyme books or tapes to share.

Practitioners could:

- ✳ put a new action rhyme on the parents and staff notice board each week.
- ✳ revive the dressing up clothes box with some new interesting additions, such as swimwear, scarves, sunglasses. Have a full-length mirror at child height.

What I really want

Looking, pointing, using sounds & words

What are they learning?

are they
   using short phrases?
   describing?
   commenting?
   taking turns?
   pretending?
this leads to
   ✳ sharing thoughts
   ✳ making choices

Looking, pointing, using sounds & words

Movers, shakers and players

Aspect:
A Skilful Communicator

Components:
Being together
Communicating
Finding a voice

60

Just Like Me
action words

What you need
* teddies
* hats
* shoes
* gloves

What you do

1. Sit opposite the children. Start by waving your arms in the air and singing, 'Everybody do this, do this, do this, everybody do this just like me'. Encourage the children to imitate your actions.
2. Give each child a teddy and then make the teddies jump. Say 'Look Teddy's jumping' and sing 'Everybody's jumping, jumping, jumping, everybody's jumping, jump like me', encouraging the children to make their teddies jump too.
3. Put on gloves and clap hands.
4. Sing, 'Everybody's clapping'.
5. Try the shoes and stamping, the hats and nodding.

another idea:
* Try hopping, tip toes and giant strides.

Ready for more?

👋 Ask the children to suggest or name actions for the song.
👋 Try introducing fast and slow, with action words, such as crawling fast or slow.

Individual needs

☼ For children with attention difficulties, play this game individually or with one other child.

☼ Try action words and noisy toys and objects for children with visual impairment, such as banging a drum, stamping feet and so on.

Tiny Tip

✳ Think of all the action words that you might use in one particular activity, eg in the water play - splashing, washing, dripping, raining and so on.

Watch, listen, reflect

👁 Watch how much the children are relying on imitating actions and how much they understand the game.

👁 Listen for phrases using action and object words.

👁 Check out how they use the action words in other situations or other play activities.

Working together

Parents could:

★ play 'Here we go Round the Mulberry Bush' with their children.

★ encourage their child to use action words in everyday situations.

Practitioners could:

★ sing and chant to provide commentary for play, such as 'Kishan is riding, riding riding' or 'This is the way we eat our dinner, eat our dinner ...'

What I really want

Looking, pointing, using sounds & words

What are they learning?

are they
    using action
    words?
    describing?
    commenting?
    imitating words
    and actions?
this leads to
    ★ pretend play
    ★ conversation
    ★ representing

Looking, pointing, using sounds and words

Movers, shakers and players

Aspect:
A Skilful Communicator

Components:
Being together
Communicating
Finding a voice

62

Photos and Pictures
matching objects and pictures

What you need

* pictures and photos of every-day objects
* matching objects and pictures
* a shoebox or plastic box

What you do

1. Put three everyday objects, such as a toy car, book and keys in the box. Put the lid on and shake. Give it to the child to explore.
2. When they are ready, show a picture of one of the objects - say the keys and ask if they can find the object in the box. Hold the keys and picture up together and say 'Jed, look keys, same'.
3. Play on matching objects and pictures. Increase the number of objects as the child gets more confident with the matching. Encourage them to use the names of the objects naturally as part of their play.

another idea:
* Look out for simple photo picture books and match objects to these pictures.

Ready for more?

🖐 Try matching pictures to pictures. Use lotto board cards or matching pair cards.
🖐 Cover a tray or table-top with pictures and give the children a box of objects that match the pictures.

Individual needs

☼ Take a few photos of a child's familiar objects, such as shoes, cup and coat. Match these with the real objects.

☼ Try matching distinctive textures, such as sand paper, fur, foil and so on for children with visual impairment.

Tiny Tip

❋ Look out for old board books with photograph pictures. Cut these up carefully for matching.

Watch, listen, reflect

👁 Watch how children use the word and concept 'same' in different situations.

👁 Listen for short phrases and think how the children are using the language.

👁 Check carefully to see if the phrases used are the child's own or an echo of earlier phrases used by others.

Working together

Parents could:

* match pictures and objects at every opportunity, such as 'Daddy's toothbrush, your toothbrush'.
* spend a few moments every day looking at pictures and photos together.

Practitioners could:

* display pictures of everyday objects, such as clothes in the dressing up corner, washing stuff in the bathroom and so on.
* take photos of home corner toys and keep the album in the home corner to share with children.

What I really want

Looking, pointing, using sounds and words

What are they learning?

are they
matching?
using object words?
describing?
sharing fun?
this leads to
* exploring
* experimenting
* learning about words

Looking, pointing, using sounds and words

Movers, shakers and players

Aspect:
A Skilful Communicator

Components:
Being together
Communicating
Finding a voice

64

Up and Down
words and actions

What you need
* 1m square of fabric, bubble wrap, net or survival blanket (from a camping shop)
* beach ball or balloon

What you do
Play this game with one or two children.
1. Stand opposite them and give them each a corner of the fabric square. Hold the other two corners yourself. Pull the fabric taut.
2. Bend low and then stretch as high as the children can reach wafting the fabric up and down together. Sing or chant together, 'Up and down, up and down, up and down and stop'. Do this fast and then slow.
3. Carefully balance the ball on the fabric and have some fun bouncing the ball or balloon up and down as you repeat the rhyme and actions.
4. Play again with the bubble wrap and other materials.

another idea:
* Put a teddy on the square and bounce him up and down.

Ready for more?
✋ Try 'The Grand Old Duke of York', with up and down actions.
✋ Make huge up and down movements with big brushes and paint on large sheets of paper. Sing as you paint.

Individual needs

✿ Sew a plastic bangle to the corners of the fabric square to make an easier grip for children with fine motor difficulties.

✿ If it is hard to hold the attention of a child, sit opposite them and try the rhyme and actions holding hands.

Tiny Tip

❋ Survival blankets are inexpensive, and are huge, so they can be easily divided up into several smaller blankets.

Watch, listen, reflect

👁 Watch how the children play together. How are they communicating with each other?

👁 Think about words, actions, gesture, body language and so on.

👁 Listen for short phrases, describing words and comments.

Working together

Parents could:

* use up and down in some gentle active play with their child.
* try this rhyme with some bouncing on the knee games.

Practitioners could:

* look out at the local library for finger and action rhyme books and tapes.
* talk to parents about the different ways their child is using language, with real examples.

What I really want

Looking, pointing, using sounds and words

What are they learning?

are they
    having fun?
    enjoying being with others?
    using words and actions?
    exploring?
this leads to
    * communicating
    * negotiating
    * collaborating

Movers, shakers and players

Aspect:
A Skilful Communicator

Components:
Finding a voice

After You!
turn taking with an object

What you need

* a basket of small familiar everyday objects
  Choose ones that the children can name.

What you do

1. Sit on the floor with two or three children.
2. Tip out the basket of objects, name each one and check that the children know what each one is called.
3. Now start by asking each child in turn to give you a named object. Say 'Name, can you give me the spoon?'. Give them time and praise them, whatever they give you. If they give you the wrong thing, say 'Thank you. Now can you give me the spoon?' If they get it right, say 'Thank you, you gave me the spoon.'
4. Continue until each child has had several turns.

another idea:
* Play again with a basket of soft toys, cups and saucers, vehicles or animals.

Ready for more?

- Use a selection of objects all the same but different colours (eg bricks, beakers, balls). Ask for a red ball, a green beaker.
- Play this game with pictures of objects.

66

Individual needs

⚙ Try with a group of object picture pairs and ask them to find the pair and give it to you.

⚙ For children with special interests, try including some objects or pictures related to their particular interest.

Tiny Tip

✳ Add one unfamiliar object as children get used to this game. Introduce the new name as you start the game.

Watch, listen, reflect

👁 Note any new words they are using, and any names they don't understand or know.

👁 Play the game with one child only if they find a small group difficult.

👁 Observe how they watch and learn from each other, learning to take turns.

Working together

Parents could:

* play this game at home with familiar toys, etc.
* extend their child's first words - if the child says 'Dog', reply with 'Yes, it's a dog'.

Practitioners could:

* encourage and model using the child's name first, to gain attention, when talking to young children.
* observe children and tell parents about new interests and games they have been playing.

What's that?

Making sounds, naming, questioning

What are they learning?

are they
  naming objects?
  understanding requests and instructions?
  taking turns?

this leads to
  * understanding object names
  * following instructions

Making sounds, naming, questioning

Movers, shakers and players

Aspect:
A Skilful Communicator

Components:
Finding a voice

What's This?
naming objects

What you need

* a small basket or a handful of familiar objects
* one or two children

What you do

1. Sit on the floor with the child or children.
2. Tip out the basket of objects and help them to explore them, naming them as they play.
3. Ask the child (or one child at a time) to put an object back in the basket. Say '*Name*, can you put the glove in the basket?'
4. If they put a different object in, take it out and say, 'Good try, can you find the glove?'
5. Continue putting objects in the basket until they are all back.
6. If they are enjoying the game, tip the basket out and start again.

another idea:
* Play the game with pretend fruit, vehicles, animals, etc.

Ready for more?

🖐 Use a collection of identical objects of different colours - bricks, cups, pens, etc. Ask them to return by colour and object.
🖐 Play with children giving you instructions.

Individual needs

☼ Start with a small number of objects and ones that are really familiar to the child.

☼ Work with one child until you are really sure they can engage with the game in a small group.

☼ Use bright and easy to grasp objects.

Tiny Tip

❋ You could let the children make the collection of objects for the game.

Watch, listen, reflect

👁 Note any objects they find difficult to locate and name.

👁 Observe children's faces and eyes when they are locating objects.

👁 Watch to see if the children are listening to and watching each other!

Working together

Parents could:

* use familiar toys and objects at home for naming games.

* tell practitioners about new words their children have learned.

Practitioners could:

* explain why this game is important in language development.

* offer simple object collections in the toy library.

What's that?

Making sounds, naming, questioning

What are they learning?

are they
   listening?
   saying names of objects?
   taking turns?
   looking?

this leads to
   * new vocabulary
   * improved listening

Making sounds, naming, and questioning

Movers, shakers and players

Aspect:
A Skilful Communicator

Components:
Finding a voice

70

Animal Antics
animal noises

What you need

* a selection of small world domestic and farm animals (plastic or wooden) - several of each animal
* farm play mat, fences, sheds, etc. (optional)

What you do

1. Work with two or three children.
2. Take the animals out of the basket and look at them. Talk about their names and the sounds they make.
3. Work together to stand all the animals up on the table or play mat, making the sound for each as you do.
4. Sing, 'I went to visit a farm one day, and saw a cow/pig/cat/horse along the way.' *Pause and let each child find the correct animal.* 'What do you think I heard it say?' *All add the appropriate animal noise* eg. 'Moo, moo, moo.'
5. Continue to sing the song with different animals.

another idea:
* Make a farm scene and move the animals about, making the appropriate noises as they go.

Ready for more?

☝ Play the game with Old MacDonald had a Farm.

☝ Put animals in a feely bag and ask the children to make the noise for the animal they take out of the bag.

Individual needs

☼ Start with two or three animals which are familiar to the child.

☼ You could use a tape recording of animal noises to help children who have language or speech difficulties, and those who have English as an additional language.

Tiny Tip

✳ Make a scrapbook of pictures of animals in a photo or display book with plastic wallet pages.

Watch, listen, reflect

👁 Listen to the animal sounds they are making.

👁 Watch how they look for and identify the animals.

👁 Listen to children playing freely with the animals and note the use of new sounds and names of the animals.

Working together

Parents could:

* play 'Animal Spotting' or 'Animal Antics' at home or when they are out.
* share books and watch TV programmes about animals.
* visit farm parks, city farms, zoos or safari parks and talk about animal names and noises.

Practitioners could:

* offer animal sets and simple animal picture books as part of the toy library.
* encourage families to talk about their visits, pets and animals they see.

What's that?

Making sounds, naming, and questioning

What are they learning?

are they
    using animal noises?
    looking carefully?
    learning new words and sounds?

this leads to
    * pretend play
    * descriptions
    * recognising

Making sounds,
naming, and
questioning

**Movers, shakers
and players**

Aspect:
A Skilful
Communicator

Components:
Finding a voice

72

I Say, You Say, I Do, You Do
copying words and movements

What you need

* no special equipment

What you do

1. Sit in a circle with two or three children.
2. When everyone is ready, explain the game, which is about copying what you say or do.
3. Start with some simple sounds *(eg. popping lips, Ahhh, single words, numbers)* and movements *(eg. hands on head, finger on lips, stand on one leg, stand up then sit down, funny faces)*.
4. You do something, they must copy it. Alternate sounds and movements.
5. Give plenty of praise for good copying.

another idea:

* Let one child be the leader, making sounds or movements for the others to copy.

Ready for more?

🖐 Try making a sound <u>with</u> a movement.
🖐 Use very small movements, so they have to watch you carefully.
🖐 Make series of sounds, several words together or sing one line of a song.

Individual needs

- ✿ Start with one child, using movements that can easily be copied, such as clapping, opening your mouth, single sounds.
- ✿ Cut some pictures of faces from magazines and use them for copying expressions.

Tiny Tip

✻ Play this game outside in the garden or during group time to fill odd minutes.

Watch, listen, reflect

- 👁 Observe how children watch and concentrate.
- 👁 Note any movements they find difficult.
- 👁 Watch to see if the child copies you or waits for others in the group and copies them.
- 👁 Do some children find sounds more difficult to copy than movements?

Working together

Parents could:

- * play the 'I say, you say' game at home.
- * look for some 'find the pairs' pictures in comics and children's magazines.
- * play and sing 'Put your Finger in the Air' or 'Heads, Shoulders, Knees and Toes'.

Practitioners could:

- * add some matching pairs or pelmanism games to the toy library. You can make these from wrapping paper pictures, magazine photos or digital photos of your setting.

What's that?

Making sounds, naming, and questioning

What are they learning?

are they
 looking at you?
 copying?
 responding?
 sharing fun?
this leads to
 * concentration
 * taking turns
 * observation

Movers, shakers and players

Aspect:
A Skilful Communicator

Components:
Finding a voice

Bedtime Dolly!
talking about sequences of actions

What you need
* a doll with clothes and pyjamas or a change of clothes
* doll's bed with blankets, etc

What you do
Play this game with one or two children. You could play in the home area.

1. Sit with the children and talk about the doll. What is he/she wearing? What are the names of his/her clothes?
2. Now suggest that it is time for the doll to go to bed. Ask the children what happens when you go to bed. Use the words 'next' and 'after' to help them get a sense of sequence. Practice any new words.
3. Now help the children to go through the bedtime sequence with the baby, undressing it, putting on night clothes, washing face, cleaning teeth, story time, etc.
4. Sing a quiet song to the baby to send it to sleep.

another idea:
* Make a sequencing game by taking photos of this activity.

Ready for more?
- Let the children re-play this activity in the role play area.
- Provide a child sized bed time kit, so the children can play going to bed. Add washing things, stories, a song tape of lullabies.

74

Individual needs

☼ Keep the sequence to two or three actions for children with language difficulties.

☼ Use sequencing cards or symbols to help children understand before and after. Start with just two or three cards.

Tiny Tip

✳ Fleece makes lovely blankets and it doesn't need hemming! Use a thin fleece so children can manage it easily.

Watch, listen, reflect

👁 Listen for children's ideas about what happens first, next, after.

👁 Note any new words they are using to describe processes like washing or undressing.

👁 Watch for examples of children copying the behaviour of their parents or other adults, learning from these models.

Working together

Parents could:

* talk through sequences as they happen - laying the table, getting a meal, having a bath, getting ready to go out, etc.
* join in children's pretend play and sometimes be the baby!

Practitioners could:

* find some simple books that have sequences of familiar events – such as shopping, going to the park, preparing for a visit, etc.
* encourage parents to join children in their role play, and to try not to dominate what happens.

What's that?

Making sounds, naming, and questioning

What are they learning?

are they
    remembering?
    copying?
    using words and
    actions?
    sequencing ideas?

this leads to
    * role play
    * more complex
      sequences
    * story telling

Movers, shakers and players

Aspect:
A Skilful Communicator

Components:
Listening and responding

More Than One
finding, matching and first sorting

What you need

* two each of a selection of everyday objects, such as toy cars, books, balls, dustpan and brushes, sponges, bricks, wooden spoons, etc.
* a large cloth

What you do

1. Spread the pairs of everyday objects out on the cloth. Ask each child to choose an object. Now see if you can all find another of the same.
2. Talk about the different objects and pretend to use them. Use action words as well as object words.
3. Next, hide all the objects under the cloth. Lie down around the edge and feel under the cloth to see what objects you can find. Any pairs? Remember, no peeking!

another idea:

* Play this game with lots of cars, bricks and books. See if the children can pull all the cars out from under the cloth, all the books, all the bricks and so on by feel alone.

Ready for more?

✋ Practice sorting cutlery into a cutlery tray, all the spoons together, all the forks and so on.
✋ Make a pile of bricks and toy cars. Pull out all the cars to make a traffic jam, and all the bricks to make a tower

Individual needs

☼ Start with just two or three pairs of very familiar everyday objects, such as cup, toy car and shoe, for children at an early developmental stage.

☼ Use natural gesture and pointing to provide clues and prompts to help children's emerging understanding of language.

Tiny Tip

✳ Sort and store every day objects near where they are used, so children can link objects and use.

Watch, listen, reflect

👁 Look to see if children understand the use of the objects, as well as their name labels.

👁 Listen for first words, object words as well as action words.

👁 Watch to see if children understand the concept of 'same'.

👁 Can the children relate the objects used in the activity to other objects they see around them?

Working together

Parents could:

★ help their child to sort and match into pairs a pile of socks.

★ look for photograph books of everyday objects and share these with their child, using object and action words.

Practitioners could:

★ share with parents how first words and early understanding are encouraged in the setting.

★ put up a poster with ideas of what to look for when choosing picture books and storybooks, with details of the local library.

Let's listen

Listening to learn & learning to listen

What are they learning?

are they
using object names?
finding the same?
using sounds and gesture together?
this leads to
* using first words and phrases
* following simple rules

Movers, shakers and players

Aspect:
A Skilful Communicator

Components:
Listening and responding

Clap, Clap, Stamp, Stamp
imitating actions and sounds

What you need

* a basket of gloves
* some wrist toys

What you do

1. With the gloves and wrist toys out of sight, sit with two or three children on the floor. Using a tune you are comfortable with and actions to accompany the words, sing:
   I have two hands to clap, clap, clap, clap,
   I have two feet to stamp, stamp, stamp, stamp
   Clap, clap, clap, stamp, stamp, stamp.
2. Now, let the children choose some gloves, and sing the rhyme and do the actions again with you.
3. Next, offer the children the wrist toys to wear on their ankles! Try the rhyme again.

another idea:

* Try it with an odd assortment of dressing up footwear, perhaps fluffy slippers, wellington boots, tap shoes or even flippers!

Ready for more?

🖐 Vary the pace of the song. Try it very quickly and then very, very slowly.

🖐 Play stamping games outside in puddles, on gravel, on grass on the path.

Individual needs

☼ Match the actions of the song to the physical abilities of children within the group.

☼ Encourage children with fine motor difficulties to bring two hands to the midline.

☼ Keep the game short and lively for children with attention difficulties.

Tiny Tip

✳ Sew small bells securely onto elastic for some quick, easy and effective wrist toys.

Watch, listen, reflect

👁 Watch to see if the children are remembering the rhyme and actions, anticipating the next action.

👁 Watch how they make and express choices of gloves and wrist toys.

👁 Listen to the range of sounds and single words they are using.

👁 Think about how they imitate other actions during the day, perhaps in simple pretend play.

Working together

Parents could:

* try some new action rhymes with their child.
* add a few minutes of rhymes to bedtime routine.

Practitioners could:

* create a book of favourite action rhymes for loan to parents.
* talk to parents about the importance of imitation in early learning, and the sorts of opportunities for imitation offered within the setting.

Let's listen

Understanding & being understood

What are they learning?

are they
  imitating actions?
  using action words?
  enjoying being in a small group?
  making choices?
this leads to
  * listening skills
  * joining in with action rhymes

Movers, shakers and players

Aspect:
A Skilful Communicator

Components:
Listening and responding

In it Goes
posting objects and pictures

What you need

* picture-pairs games
* cardboard tubes, such as potato snack tubes
* scissors, glue, red paper and a black marker pen

What you do

1. Cut a posting slot in the tube. Cover the tube with red paper to make a simple posting box. Use the marker pen to add some details and highlight the edge of the posting slot.
2. Choose six different cards, starting with pictures of familiar objects. Spread the cards face down on the floor or table.
3. Take turns with the child to choose a card. Give them time to name the card. If they don't attempt to name it, say for example, 'Name, look, card'. Post the card into the box and say 'Card gone'.
4. Take turns. Talk about the pictures and relate them to objects you can see around you in your setting.

another idea:
* Make a larger post box and post real everyday objects.

Ready for more?

🖐 Turn the cards face up and ask the child to find a card by name, such as 'Where's the flower?' then post it.
🖐 Ask older children to take turns to tell <u>you</u> which card to find.

Individual needs

☼ For children at an early developmental level, use real objects or photographs of real objects.

☼ Use real objects and a bright yellow posting box for children with visual difficulties.

☼ accept different ways of responding.

Tiny Tip

✻ Give the game a definite end, such as shaking the post box and then tipping all the cards back into the pairs box.

Watch, listen, reflect

👁 Note if they understand single object words. Do they show understanding of the use of the objects?

👁 Listen for attempts at first words, and sounds combined with gestures and pointing.

👁 Consider each child's understanding of language, as well as their expressive language.

Working together

Parents could:

* spend a few minutes every day looking at books and pictures with their child.
* talk about pictures they see as they go out and about together.

Practitioners could:

* make sure that a good range of picture books is available and update these regularly.
* check the picture-pairs and lotto games in the setting to ensure different styles of images, photographs and line drawings are available.

Let's listen

Listening to learn and learning to listen

What are they learning?

are they
    understanding
    first words and
    simple rules?
    listening?
    taking turns?
    attending?
this leads to
    * attention
    * taking part in a
       simple game

81

Movers, shakers and players

Aspect:
A Skilful Communicator

Components:
Listening and responding

Give Me a Clue
understanding daily routines and sequences

What you need

* a camera
* card and a marker pen

What you do

1. Make a list of the main activities and routines within the setting, such as meals, snacks, group time, different play activities, looking at books going outside.
2. Take photographs of each of these activities. Mount these on card and use the marker pen to add simple line drawing borders which add additional clues, such as on the photo of the tray of cups, add a border of milk bottles, water jugs, straws, etc.
3. Show some of the photos to the children. Talk about them and use these photographs to help children know what is happening next, such as showing them the 'Dinner time' photo card, when it is time to get ready.
4. Also, use the cards to help the children make choices about what they want to play with or put outside.

Ready for more?

🖐 Make a visual timetable for older children by fixing the photos to the wall in the order in which they will occur that day. As each activity passes, take that photo down.

Individual needs

☼ Use objects rather than photographs as prompts for visually impaired children and those at an early developmental stage.

☼ For children with fine motor difficulties, make sure the photographs are mounted on chunky card, and shaped for easy grip.

Tiny Tip

✳ Make sure all practitioners in the setting use the child's name first when talking to individuals.

Watch, listen, reflect

👁 Listen for attempts at first words, object and action words to describe the images.

👁 Watch how individual children relate the photographs to activities and routines.

👁 Watch to see how children find details in the pictures. Look for pointing and natural gesture.

Working together

Parents could:

* bring in photos of their child and family for practitioners to share with the child.
* talk to children about what is happening next, giving them clues and reminders to help early understanding.

Practitioners could:

* talk to parents about how understanding of language emerges from everyday objects, experiences and routines.
* develop a poster or fact sheet for parents with ideas of what could be done at home to support language development.

Let's listen

Listening to learn and learning to listen

What are they learning?

are they
    using object names, first words and phrases?
    using clues and prompts?
    making choices?
    listening?
this leads to
    * sustained attention

83

Movers, shakers and players

Aspect:
A Skilful Communicator

Components:
Making meaning

84

My Turn, Your Turn
taking turns in actions

What you need

* a selection of sound makers - shakers, bells, buzzers, electronic or battery toys with buttons, buzzers or beepers

What you do

Work with one child, unless they are already good at turn taking. Then you could play with two, but keep the group small!

1. Put the objects on the floor between you.
2. Experiment with the sounds they make. Show the child how to make the sounds if they need help.
3. Now choose one of the sound makers each, and take turns making your sound. Wait for them to make the sound, then make yours. Wait again, do it again. You may need to make an exaggerated 'Oh' as you each take a turn. Encourage the child to wait for their turn - they may find this difficult until they get the hang of the game.

another idea:
* Take turns putting pegs round the edge of a tin, bricks in a posting box, buttons in a jar.

Ready for more?

* Plan lots of little turn taking games in one-to-one situations.
* Play 'Pass the toy', when you are changing children.
* Sit opposite a child and pass an object through a tube, a small hoop etc

Individual needs

☼ Start with one object, perhaps a noise-making toy. Put it between you and take turns making the noise.

☼ Try turn taking with a marker, making marks in gloop or foam, dropping a brick into a noisy tin, poking a finger into dough or sticking a little sticker on a mirror.

Tiny Tip

✽ Turn taking in actions supports turn taking in conversations. Waiting, listening, looking are all part of making meaning.

Watch, listen, reflect

👁 Watch to see if children can wait for their turn.

👁 Look for increasing enjoyment in these simple games.

👁 Note how well the child listens and watches.

👁 Note any child who finds waiting impossible. They will need more practice in these simple games.

Working together

Parents could:

* play simple turn-taking games when clearing up toys and clothes.
* make a turn taking game with voices and faces - making pops, mouth and tongue noises, expressions, 'blowing raspberries' etc.

Practitioners could:

* explain to parents that taking turns is not just about sharing equipment, taking turns is at the heart of good communication and active listening.
* model being a good listener with parents and colleagues as well as with children.

Get the message

Understanding and being understood

What are they learning?

are they
  watching?
  listening?
  taking turns?
  enjoying a game?
this leads to
  * turn taking in conversations
  * listening
  * making sounds and words

Movers, shakers and players

Aspect:
A Skilful Communicator

Components:
Making meaning

Decisions, Decisions!
sharing choices

What you need

* a table covered with paper, stuck down, so it won't move
* lots of large felt pens or crayons

What you do

This is a free choice activity about choosing, negotiating, working together. Work with two or three children to start with, then leave the activity out for the whole session so more children can join in.

1. Put the mark makers on the table. Children need to stand up.
2. Watch the children as they start to make marks on the paper, moving around as they do so.
3. Help them with pen tops etc. if they need it, but don't direct what they do to the paper.
4. Use a running commentary to describe what they are doing. Encourage talk, negotiation and selection. Listen as children describe what they are doing and the marks they are making, the colours they are choosing.

another idea: * Try the activity with paint or glue and spreaders.

Ready for more?

- Provide big chalk boards or water painting outside, so children have to negotiate and work together.
- Plan collaborative brick building, small world, so children can develop social and verbal skills.

Individual needs

✿ Children with behavioural difficulties often find collaborative work difficult. Help them by doing some of these activities with an adult before negotiating with other children.

✿ Children with developmental delay may need reduced choice to make this activity work.

Tiny Tip

❋ Always offer some collaborative play and a wide choice of equipment for mark making and creative work.

Watch, listen, reflect

👁 Watch to see how well the children work together, share and take turns.

👁 Watch how they manage the pens, pen tops etc, and how their fine motor control is developing.

👁 Listen to the range of sounds and single words they are using as they work together.

Working together

Parents could:

★ try this game with bath crayons, working with their child to make a picture.

★ try sharing out books, toys, raisins, so children begin to share and negotiate. Use words like 'Mine', 'yours', 'shar'e', 'turns'.

Practitioners could:

★ display the outcomes of the activity where parents can see it; adding an explanation of what children are learning.

★ regularly include collaborative activities and opportunities in their planning.

Get the message

Understanding and being understood

What are they learning?

are they
    talking?
    selecting?
    enjoying being in a small group?
    aware of others?
this leads to
    * collaboration
    * negotiation
    * taking turns

Understanding and being understood

Movers, shakers and players

Aspect:
A Skilful Communicator

Components:
Making meaning

Lets Eat!
making a simple snack

What you need
* bread; toaster (if possible)
* butter or spread
* blunt knives (little butter knives are perfect)
* spreads (Marmite, fruit spread, paste etc.)

What you do
1. Work with two or three children on this early snack activity. You could make sandwiches or toast (toast is easier for small spreaders!). They could sit or stand up.
2. Make some toast or offer some bread to the children. Half or quarter slices are easiest to start with.
3. Keep the spreads and toppings near you to start with, so children have to ask you for them.
4. Work with the children to spread butter or spread on their own toast. Talk as you all work. Encourage them to ask for the things they want. Use 'Please' and 'Thank you' as you pass things to each other, and pause for answers.
5. Add toppings, asking each child what they would like.
6. Eat the toast as you spread it, and offer another piece to those who want it.

Ready for more?
🖐 Involve children in preparing and giving out snacks. Younger children can do this very well when we let them!
🖐 Children can make their own sandwiches or snacks unaided, with an adult watching.

Individual needs

- ✿ Children with physical difficulties should sit to do this activity.
- ✿ Accept gesture, pointing, signs or sounds when children with communication difficulties are choosing and negotiating.
- ✿ Give limited choices at first - and always ask the child, even if they may not appear to understand.

Tiny Tip

❋ Independent activities encourage negotiation and brain growth as well as choice. Give children as much choice as you can.

Watch, listen, reflect

- 👁 Note whether the children can choose and indicate a choice to you.
- 👁 Listen for words and sounds combined with gestures, expression and pointing.
- 👁 This activity gives you a good chance to look at and assess fine motor development. Can they manage simple tools for spreading?

Working together

Parents could:

- ∗ make opportunities for their children to ask for the things they want, and to choose from two options.
- ∗ always model the use of 'Please' and 'Thank you' when they are with their children.

Practitioners could:

- ∗ make a list of activities where children can choose and be independent. Take photos of the activities and display them where parents can see what their children can do.

Get the message

Understanding and being understood

What are they learning?

are they
concentrating?
choosing?
taking turns?
watching and
copying?
this leads to
* negotiating
* independence
* communicating
choices

89

Get the Message

Understanding and being understood

Movers, shakers and players

Aspect:
A Skilful Communicator

Components:
Makiing meaning

Who is it, What is it?
recognising and naming

What you need

* a camera
* photos of familiar objects and people

What you do

1. Take some photos of the children, adults, objects and activities in the setting.
2. Print the photos and stick them on card if they need it. Laminating the photos will make them last longer. Children love looking at photos.
3. Work with two or three children at a table or on the carpet.
4. Put the photos on the table or floor one at a time, naming the person, object or activity as you do so. Don't use too many cards at once (start with six or eight).
5. Pick up one of the cards and say '(Name) who/what is this?' Give the card to the named child to look at. If they name the object or person, they can keep the card. Continue until all the cards are gone.
6. Play again if they are keen for more.

Ready for more?

- Make small photo albums - animals, objects, people, activities.
- Make a small album for each child, with pictures of their special favourites, family, home etc.

Individual needs

☼ Make photo books or put photo books on the computer so children can find their own favourites.

☼ For children with fine motor difficulties, make sure the photographs are mounted on chunky card, and shaped for easy grip.

Tiny Tip

✳ Make sure all practitioners in the setting use the child's name first when working in small groups.

Watch, listen, reflect

👁 Listen for first words and sounds.

👁 Watch for children pointing or gesturing to the object, activity or person in the photo.

👁 Note the children who have difficulty relating pictures to objects or people. You may have to help these children by using the object and the photo together as a matching game.

Working together

Parents could:

* bring in photos of their child and family for their child's personal photo book.
* make and use photo albums and simple photo books to extend their child's vocabulary.

Practitioners could:

* lend parents disposable cameras to take pictures of their child's favourite objects and activities for their own photo book.
* put a 'Who is this?' game in the loan collection or toy library.

Get the message

Understanding and being understood

What are they learning?

are they
    watching?
    enjoying a game?
    using object names, first words and phrases?
this leads to
    * looking closely
    * turn taking
    * new words

Resources for all stages of A Skilful Communicator

Resources

toy telephones
cups
beakers
spoons
plate
clothes
pairs of socks
pairs of gloves
small baskets
dolls
dolls' clothes
cot blankets
real/plastic coins
purses and bags
paper plates
garden sticks
feely boxes/bags
tape recorder
camera
small world sets
toy vehicles
rattles
tambourines
shakers and bells

Fabrics for dressing up and games

* Try *Fabricadabra*! fabric packs and lycra squares from Featherstone Education (01858 881213)

Dressing up box list

hats	slippers	waistcoats
jewellery	ballet shoes	aprons
scarves	boots	overalls
gloves	flippers	briefcases
handbags	shirts	saris
purses	trousers	overshirts
sunglasses	shorts	glasses
baby clothes	swimwear	cloaks
shoes	large socks	skirts
wellies	coats	

Anthologies

<u>This Little Puffin</u> compiled by Elizabeth Matterson (Penguin)

<u>Bobby Shaftoe</u> by Sue Nicholls (A&C Black)

<u>Lucy Collins Big Book of Nursery Rhymes</u> illustrated by Lucy Collins (Macmillan)

<u>Okki Tokki Unga, Action Songs for Children</u> chosen by Harrop, Friend and Gadsby (A&C Black)

<u>The Little Book of Nursery Rhymes</u> compiled by Sally Featherstone (Featherstone Education)

Action Songs

Wind the Bobbin
Heads, Shoulders, Knees and Toes
Miss Polly had a Dolly
Row, Row, Row Your Boat
The Wheels on the Bus
In a Cottage in a Wood
Simon Says
I Spy with my Little Eye
I Hear with my Little Ear
Who Stole the Cookies?
Put your Finger in the Air
What's the Time Mr Wolf?

Songs to help imitation & imagination

I'm a Little Teapot
Five Currant Buns
Miss Polly had a Dolly
Row, Row, Row Your Boat
The Wheels on the Bus
Dingle Dangle Scarecrow
Little Peter Rabbit
Here we go Round the Mulberry Bush
There was a Princess Long Ago
In Cottage in a Wood
I Can Play on the Big Bass Drum
I Went to Visit the Farm One Day

Everyday objects

keys
cup
spoon
plate
hat
shoe
car
bus
flannel
brush
toothbrush
sponge
sock
purse
dog
cat
book
telephone
bowl
basket
toy tele-
phones
cups
beakers
spoons
plates
clothes

dolls
dolls'
clothes
cot blankets
plastic coins
purses bags
paper plates
garden
sticks
tape
recorder
camera
toy vehicles
rattles
shakers bells

pairs of
gloves
socks
shoes
trainers
boots
chopsticks
drumsticks
cymbals
shakers

For music and movement

shakers
bells
drums
castanets
rattles
sticks
chime bars
tins
cans
old
saucepans
metal teapots
spoons

tambourines
gloves
cloaks
shoes
ribbons
balloons
lycra squares
and strips
gauze
net
feathers
bubbles
foam

Pictures of objects and people

Collect some pictures of objects and faces (use catalogues, magazines, old books, brochures) and real objects that match. Take some photos of objects in your setting and put them with the real object.
Take some photos of the people in your setting and outside to recognise and name.
Always ask permission before photographing anyone!

Resources:
A Skilful Communicator

93

Section 3

The Following section contains activities for young children, to help build **a Competent Learner**

The relevant Birth to Three Matters components are:
* **Being Imaginative**
* **Being Creative**
* **Making Connections**
* **Representing**

Touch it - feel it

Sensory play through touch

Movers, shakers and players

Aspect:
A Competent Learner

Components:
Being imaginative
Being creative

96

Bubble & Blow
feeling bubbles and air

What you need
* bubbles and blowers
* straws
* small battery powered fans
* one or two children

What you do
1. Collect the equipment.
2. Talk to the children about the bubbles and blowers.
3. Let them experiment with bubble blowers and straws.
4. Work alongside the children, blowing bubbles, talking about what they look like and what they do - words like 'float, colour, air, move, spin, land, pop, burst'.
5. Use the straws to blow the bubble mixture and to blow gently on hands, arms, cheeks.
6. Try catching the bubbles on hands and arms.
7. Use the battery fans (or a hair drier) to blow the bubbles around or to blow gently on skin and hair. Talk about what it feels like.

another idea:
* Try these activities outside on a calm day.

Ready for more?
🖐 Use wire coat hangers or bendy twigs to make giant bubbles with mixture in a washing up bowl.
🖐 Make some foamy water with bubble bath and play scooping and blowing the foam.

Individual needs

- ☼ Blowing gently on skin with a straw or fan is a great stimulus for babies and older children.
- ☼ Blowing bubbles really relaxes children and gets their attention.
- ☼ Watch for responses of pleasure - eye movements, wriggling, turning.

Safety Tip
❋ Cut a little nick near the top of the straw to prevent accidental swallowing of bubble stuff.

Watch, listen, reflect

- 👁 Listen, and praise the use of sounds and words.
- 👁 Watch how children respond to the bubbles and the air on their skin.
- 👁 Watch for hand or other movements in imitation of the floating bubbles.
- 👁 Praise physical movements and control.

Working together

Parents could:

- ✳ use bubbles and straws to help children become more skilful and articulate at home.
- ✳ use bath time for learning with bubbles, straws, tubing, etc.

Practitioners could:

- ✳ take some photos of this activity so parents can see what fun it is and what children are learning.
- ✳ encourage parents to use descriptive words when they are playing with children.

Touch it - feel it

Sensory play through touch

What are they learning?

are they
  exploring?
  sensing on skin?
  looking?
  sharing?
  using words?
  using sounds?
  describing
this leads to
  ✳ imagining
  ✳ comparing

Sensory play
through touch

Movers, shakers
and players

Aspect:
A Competent
Learner

Components:
Being imaginative
Being creative

Crinkle, Crackle and Pop
materials that make sounds

What you need
* a range of different sorts of
  flexible papers and other
  textured materials - foil,
  bubble wrap, tissue, chocolate
  box liners, cellophane
* one or two children

What you do
1. Put the materials on a table or the floor (the floor is
   best!).
2. Sit with the children and explore the materials together.
3. Talk about the feel of the materials, and the sounds they
   make - model the descriptive words - shiny, crinkle,
   crackly.
4. Model and encourage descriptions of what they feel like
   and sound like - 'Feels like a mirror,' 'Feels like my rain-
   coat' or 'Sounds like rain,' 'Sounds like fireworks.'
5. Pat, squash, walk, stamp, jump on the materials (with
   bare feet if possible).

another idea:
* Pin or staple some pieces of the materials to squares of
  card or a low level pinboard, and use for feeling & matching.

Ready for more?
🖐 Spread big pieces of
   bubble wrap on the
   floor (indoors or
   outside) for jumping
   or rolling on.
🖐 Squish foil into shapes
   or balls, push tissue
   paper through the
   opening of a tissue box

Individual needs

☼ Put textured papers on chair trays or over cushions.

☼ Help children to touch and feel the papers by placing them under or very near their hands.

☼ Talk through the activity, using encouraging and describing words.

Tiny Tip

✳ Try fake grass, sand or carpet for bare foot walking.

Watch, listen, reflect

👁 Watch for fine motor movements of fingers, hands, fists, feet.

👁 Listen for imitation of the sounds the materials make.

👁 Listen for any comparisons 'Like bubbles', 'Popping'.

👁 Note their enjoyment and willingness to experiment.

👁 Notice and praise effort.

Working together

Parents could:

✳ enjoy playing with textures and sounds at home, using packaging, wrapping paper, etc.

✳ bring in packaging from work and home.

✳ join in bubble wrap jumping sessions.

Practitioners could:

✳ make sure parents know how important it is for children to explore with their whole bodies.

✳ share the fun with parents, and include them in watching the children.

Touch it - feel it

Sensory play through touch

What are they learning?

are they
   exploring?
   feeling?
   looking?
   sharing?
   making sounds?
   listening?
   moving?
this leads to
   ✳ imitating
   ✳ comparing

**Movers, shakers
and players**

Aspect:
A Competent
Learner

Components:
Being imaginative
Being creative

Bury & Build
experiencing sand

What you need

* clean, dry silver sand
* a tray or shallow container
* one or two children
* small objects or toys to bury
  (eg big beads, toy cars,
  bricks, play people, etc.)

What you do

1. Put a shallow layer of sand in the container.
2. Put the container on the floor between you.
3. Encourage the children to explore the sand, scooping and letting it run through their fingers, pushing, raking, sifting, piling with their hands. Lift some high and let it fall.
4. Talk about what the sand feels and looks like.
5. Continue for a few minutes, until they have had enough.
6. Now bury some small objects in the sand. Let the children see what you are doing. You may need to add more sand.
7. Dig in the sand and see what you can find.

another idea:
* Bury some toys and feel for them with closed eyes. Guess what you have found.

Ready for more?

🖐 Mix dry pasta shapes, smaller beads etc. in the sand and sift them out with your hands.
🖐 Get the children to bury things for each other - or for you to find. Play again with your eyes closed.

Individual needs

☼ Use small individual trays such as plant saucers or seed trays for individual sand work.

☼ Give children plenty of time to play freely and explore sand before adding anything else.

☼ Try damp sand as well.

Tiny Tip

✳ Even small babies can enjoy sand play if it is well supervised.

Watch, listen, reflect

👁 Watch how they use their hands and fingers to explore the sand.

👁 Listen for and note any words or phrases they use.

👁 Praise any effort to find the buried objects, and particularly any effort to name them.

👁 Note ability to take turns and be aware of another child.

Working together

Parents could:

* play bury and find in the garden or the park.
* try putting soft toys or other objects under a blanket or the duvet for a bedtime game.
* encourage children to name what they can feel.

Practitioners could:

* encourage parents to share sand play with their children.
* offer small bags of sand for home play.
* invite parents to watch sand play in your setting.

Touch it - feel it

Sensory play through touch

What are they learning?

are they
   exploring?
   feeling?
   looking?
   sharing?
   making sounds?
   responding?
   guessing?
this leads to
   * imitating
   * comparing

Touch it - feel it

Sensory play through touch

Movers, shakers and players

Aspect:
A Competent Learner

Components:
Being imaginative
Being creative

Slip & Slide
finger painting

What you need

* finger paint (one colour is enough)
* a smooth flat surface (a table top, tray or plastic sheet)
* one or two children

see resource list on page 130 for finger paint recipes

What you do

Children usually find it easier to do this standing up.
1. Protect the children's clothing!
2. Tip some finger paint onto the smooth surface. Each child needs their own pool of paint and their own space.
3. Encourage the children to put their hands in the paint and move them around.
4. Watch and encourage, try not to interfere with their exploration of the paint.
5. Talk gently about the slipping and sliding of the paint and how it moves over the surface. Use slidey slipping sounds as you talk, and encourage them to make sounds too.

another idea:
* Try pouring out small pools of different colours.

Ready for more?

* Try putting sand in the paint.
* Paint on a big mirror or clear perspex. Or use a big piece of plastic fixed to a frame (like the child in the Birth to Three Matters video).

Individual needs

✿ Start with a small amount of paint, perhaps just enough to cover their finger tips.

✿ Try putting perfumed oils in the paint for an extra sensation.

✿ Hold a mirror in front of the child so they can see as they paint.

Tiny Tip

✳ Making your own finger paint is much cheaper and much more fun!

Watch, listen, reflect

👁 Watch how they use their hands, wrists and fingers.

👁 Look for enjoyment and involvement in the activity.

👁 Listen for sounds and words.

👁 Praise physical movements and control.

👁 Watch for patterns and squiggles emerging.

Working together

Parents could:

* let their children use finger paints at home - bath time is a good time, the paint can easily be washed off tiles and bodies!
* find out why finger painting is important to children's development.

Practitioners could:

* offer finger paint (or recipes) to parents for use at home.
* add finger paints and trays to toy library choices.
* explain what children are learning in this activity.

Touch it - feel it

Sensory play through touch

What are they learning?

are they
    exploring?
    feeling?
    looking?
    sharing?
    making patterns?
    responding?
    inventing?
this leads to
    * imagining
    * comparing

Count with me

Pattern, shape, early counting

Movers, shakers and players

Aspect:
A Competent Learner

Components:
Making connections

Discovery Fun
will it fit?

What you need

* cardboard tubes of different sizes (see tiny tip opposite)
* toy cars, bricks and balls

What you do

1. Sit with the child on the floor and explore all the tubes. Bang them, rub them together, tap your fingers on the end, blow and peek through them. Sing down the tube.
2. Bring out the balls. Give the child plenty of time to explore them. Roll them through the tubes.
3. Add the cars and bricks. Talk about what the child is doing, providing a simple commentary with short phrases.
4. Give them plenty of time to try out their ideas. Watch to see what they are discovering about how the tubes and the toys fit together.

another idea:

* Play with the tubes in the sand. Add shells – some small enough to slide through the tubes, some too large.

Ready for more?

🖐 Add sponges and cloths to the tubes in some bubbly water.
🖐 Roll balls down flexible tubing, available from DIY stores.
🖐 Make beds for toys in different boxes - a tiny teddy in a tiny box.

Individual needs

☼ Play this game at a table, with the child well supported.

☼ For those with fine motor difficulties, encourage use of two hands. Choose boxes etc. that can be manipulated easily.

☼ Allow plenty of time and repetition. Model the activity and let them watch.

Safety Tip

✳ Try tennis ball and badminton shuttle tubes or snack tubes.

Watch, listen, reflect

👁 Watch the way children manipulate the objects and how they are making discoveries.

👁 Observe how children use gesture to support their first words.

👁 Listen for first words and two word phrases. Model appropriate first words to label the objects – also concept words such as 'big', or perhaps 'gone'.

Working together

Parents could:

* save boxes and tubes for play at home and in your setting (snack tubes and sweet tubes are useful).
* try different bath toys, such as colanders, sieves, funnels, sponges and so on.

Practitioners could:

* allow plenty of time for exploratory play with natural or junk materials.
* spend time stacking and nesting boxes and bricks, varying the scale from small to very large and adding different materials, eg. corrugated card.

Count with me

Pattern, shape, early counting

What are they learning?

are they
exploring how objects fit together?
trying things out?
responding?
using fingers?

this leads to
* understanding size & volume
* using language

Movers, shakers and players

Aspect:
A Competent Learner

Components:
Making connections

106

Sort it Out
exploring same and different

What you need

* leaves
* twigs
* shells
* cones
* baskets, bowls or boxes for sorting

What you do

1. Sit together and rummage through the collection of leaves, twigs, shells and cones.
2. Allow plenty of time for unhurried exploring.
3. Choose one of the baskets and start to collect the leaves.
4. See how many you can find. Count the leaves into the basket. Feel how light the leaves are. Blow them and see them flutter. Try to draw the child's attention to the similarities. Feel the differences between the leaves, such as the shapes and textures.
5. Next collect all the cones, then the shells and sticks, sorting each into a separate basket. Tip them all out and play again. Try to follow the child's lead.

another idea:
* Sort the things and stick them in wet sand in bowls.

Ready for more?

* Sort plastic straws according to colour.
* Collect lengths of ribbon. Put all the long ones together. Put them end to end.
* Try sorting all the toy cars into different coloured traffic jams.

Individual needs

✿ Do lots of matching of everyday objects for children needing extra help.

✿ Pile up lots of soft toys, choose one teddy and ask the child to find you another one the same. Hug the teddies together.

✿ Choose objects to be sorted carefully for children with fine motor problems.

Tiny Tip

✻ Dried pasta shapes are great for sorting – all the spirals here and all the bows there!

Watch, listen, reflect

👁 Look at the way each child sorts the objects, and the strategies they use to check their sorting and correct any misplaced items.

👁 Watch how they explore objects and focus on the task in hand.

👁 Listen to the words and phrases they use and think of the purposes they are using them for.

Working together

Parents could:

* talk about same and different in everyday situations, such as 'name, look, two red buses, look the same'.

* let their child help sort out washing – all the socks here, and so on.

Practitioners could:

* check out the local toy library for sorting toys.

* ask parents to collect suitable natural objects and materials for sorting.

Count with me

Pattern, shape & early counting

What are they learning?

are they
  exploring?
  feeling?
  looking?
  sharing?
  making sounds?
  responding?
  smiling?

this leads to
  * imitating
  * comparing

Movers, shakers and players

Aspect:
A Competent Learner

Components:
Making connections

Up and Down
seesaw play

What you need

* seesaw or rocker
* soft toys

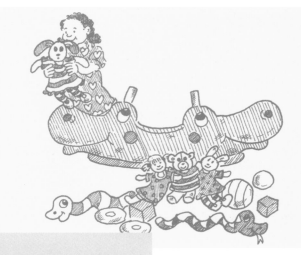

What you do

1. Help the children to choose a soft toy for each end of the rocker or see saw. Talk about how they might be feeling. 'I wonder if teddy is looking forward to his ride? Maybe he is excited, or a bit worried about it.'
2. With a child kneeling at each end of the seesaw, *gently* rock up and down. Sing 'Up and down, up and down, up and down and stop'. Stop with one end of the rocker high in the air! Then, '1,2,3, off we go... and up and down ...'
3. Now try it with just one tiny soft toy on one end and several larger ones on the other end. Talk to the children about what is happening. Encourage action words and object words.

another idea:
* Put lots of balls or balloons on a blanket. Swing the blanket.

Ready for more?

* Make some pretend see-saws for play people with card and cotton reels.
* Play with some simple balance scales, with corks, feather, shells and wooden bricks.

108

Individual needs

☼ Some children will like you to sit opposite them and gently hold their arms, call their name and swing their arms gently up and down, as you sing 'Up and down, up and down, up and down and stop'.

☼ For children with poor eye contact, play this game, but wait for a glance or eye contact before continuing.

Tiny Tip

✳ Let all the children take off their shoes, lie on their backs. You call 'up' and they wave them in the air, call 'down' and they tap them on the floor. Keep calling up and down, changing quickly!

Watch, listen, reflect

👁 Watch to see if the children are testing out their own ideas. Look at the way they are using the see-saw or rocker. Are they imitating adults' actions, watching other children, testing out their own original ideas, or playing alongside another child. What can you do to help them maintain their attention on the activity?

👁 Note the sort of language used.

Working together

Parents could:

* visit the park and play on slides, seesaws and rockers together.

* lie on the floor with their child and play at patting balloons in the air and watching them fall.

* talk about up and down, big and little, tall and short at home.

Practitioners could:

* plan an 'Up and down' song time, with rhymes such as The Grand Old Duke of York and games such as musical bumps.

Pattern, shape, early counting

What are they learning?

are they
   playing together?
   imitating?
   trying out ideas?
   using new words?

this leads to
   * investigating
   * pretend play

Movers, shakers
and players

Aspect:
A Competent
Learner

Components:
Making connections

Making Changes
wet sand play

What you need

* dry sand in a shallow tray
* corks, shells and cones
* sieves and moulds
* funnels
* plastic bottles
* water jug

What you do

1. Play alongside the children with the dry sand. Try out the moulds, and sieves. Fill the plastic bottles with dry sand. Use hands to cup the sand, fingers to sieve the sand and trickle the sand between fingers.
2. Offer the children some water from the jug. Help them to add some water to the sand. Allow them to experiment freely, making their own discoveries.
3. Talk about the different textures and the way the sand has changed. Watch carefully and imitate their actions rather than trying to direct the play.

another idea:

* Add small paper bags, or old socks and wooden spoons to damp sand.

Ready for more?

☝ Put wet sand in plastic trays or tubs, with lolly sticks and yoghurt pots for moulds. Or try ice cube trays.

☝ Try dry sand in shallow trays with paintbrushes, rollers and clean glue spatulas.

Individual needs

☼ Add some non-slip tape to the handles of sieves, wooden spoons and around the plastic bottles for children with fine motor difficulties. Non-slip mats will hold buckets and trays in place.

☼ Remember that some children may really dislike the feel of the sand on their hands. Let them use wooden spoons.

Tiny Tip

❋ Ice cube trays are great for lots of other things too. Sand play, paint, sorting tiny things.

Watch, listen, reflect

👁 Watch to see how children are using the different materials and developing their ideas.

👁 Observe what motivates the children. What can you do to help them maintain their attention?

👁 Listen for single and two word phrases. Think about the purposes for which each child is using language.

Working together

Parents could:

* try out some sensory play at home, perhaps with a washing up bowl of cooked pasta outside.

* take a walk in the park, kick leaves, feel the bark of the trees and crush fallen leaves and so on.

Practitioners could:

* look carefully at the way they plan for and use sand play.

* make a list of resources to be used with wet and dry sand, and seek parents and colleagues help with finding them.

Count with me

Pattern, shape, early counting

What are they learning?

are they
    playing together?
    feeling textures?
    looking at change?
    sharing?
    trying new words?

this leads to
    * exploring
    * describing
    * predicting

Make your mark

Early marks and writing

Movers, shakers and players

Aspect:
A Competent Learner

Components:
Representing

Dots and Spots
making marks together

What you need

* large sheets of paper; tape
* paint; big paint brushes, dabbers (sponges on sticks), small pieces of sponge

You can make dabbers by sticking sponge to sticks using Superglue (keep the tube away from children!)

What you do

This activity is suitable for groups of two to four children.
1. Tape a big sheet of paper to the wall, to a table or to the floor.
2. Put the paint in trays or shallow boxes.
3. Invite the children to make marks, dabs, streaks and patterns with the implements.
4. Stay with them and encourage them to look at the marks they are making and those of other children.
5. When they have finished, stand back and look at the creation - talk about all the patterns.

another idea:
* Put sand, sequins, lentils or flour in the paint to make it textured.

Ready for more?

* Add some toy cars to the range of implements. Run them through the paint and onto the paper.
* Try adding some small sponge rollers or washing up brushes and sponges on handles

Individual needs

○ Do this activity with one child, joining in as an equal, commenting on the marks you are both making.

○ Hold up the finished creation so they can see it from a distance. Children with additional needs often benefit from more detailed chances to look at what they have done.

Tiny tip

✳ Cut up baby sponges for really soft dabbers, and car cleaning sponges for a more chunky print.

Watch, listen, reflect

👁 Note which hand is dominant (at the moment).

👁 Look at how children are gripping the tools and implements.

👁 Listen for children talking to each other about the activity and commenting on what they are doing.

👁 Listen to what they say about the finished creation.

Working together

Parents could:

✳ use sponges to print with water or bath paint at home.

✳ let their child use a washing up sponge to make bubbly prints on the draining board or a tray.

Practitioners could:

✳ let parents see you work and notice how you stand back and let the children do the activities for themselves.

✳ collect familiar house-hold and safe junk objects for printing.

Make your mark

Early marks and writing

What are they learning?

are they
   interested and
   motivated?
   trying marks out?
   sharing a task?
   using fingers?
this leads to
   * hand control
   * creativity
   * working with
      others

Make your mark

Early marks and writing

Movers, shakers and players

Aspect:
A Competent Learner

Components:
Representing

Foaming!
making marks in shaving foam

What you need
* a can of shaving foam
* a flat surface (a table, a large tray, cement mixing tray, big safety mirror)

What you do
Activity suitable for a small group.
1. The surface for this activity needs to be flat and smooth. If you are using a tray or mirror, put it flat on the floor (or on the path outside).
2. Spray a pile of foam in front of each child.
3. Give the children plenty of time to experiment and play with the foam, spreading it, patting it, looking at their hands and fingers.
4. Join in the activity. Copy their marks and make some of your own. Don't be tempted to do symbols, letters or numbers unless the children do it first.

another idea:
* Put a drop of ready mixed paint at the edge of the foam. Watch what the children do. Talk about what happens.

Ready for more?
🖐 Offer the children some things to make marks in the spread out foam. Try glue spreaders, foam dabbers brushes and bits of stiff card.
🖐 Add aromatherapy oils for an extra sensation

114

Individual needs

☼ Less mobile children could have foam play in plant saucers or small plastic trays.
☼ Some children hate getting their hands messy - go slowly, model what to do, and start with a very small bit of foam.
☼ Always check for allergies.

Safety Tip

❊ Use an old credit card or loyalty card to clean off the foam - water just spreads it out!

Watch, listen, reflect

👁 Watch the way children experiment with the foam, how they approach it and what they do.
👁 Listen to what they say. Are they using single or two word utterances?
👁 Note their concentration. Are they enjoying the activity? Are they interacting with other children, are they talking?

Working together

Parents could:

* do some shaving foam play at home with their children.
* let their children play with washing up foam and bath bubbles.

Practitioners could:

* take some photos of these mark making activities and display them with a simple explanation of their value.
* continue to plan activities that encourage children to use both hands, as this promotes motor control.

Make your mark

Early marks and writing

What are they learning?

are they
    exploring how foam behaves?
    using their hands and fingers?
    making marks?
this leads to
    * other mark making
    * confidence in creative activities

Movers, shakers and players

Aspect:
A Competent Learner

Components:
Representing

Fingers and Thumbs
hands, fingers and paint

What you need

* a flat surface - a smooth table top is ideal
* thick paints, several colours
* thin paper for taking prints

What you do

This activity is suitable for pairs and small groups.

1. Make sure the children are well covered with aprons, as the paint often gets up their arms and onto their fronts!
2. Spoon or pour some paint in little puddles on the table.
3. Watch how the children react to the paint. Join in yourself if they are not sure how to begin - you won't have to show them twice!
4. Give them plenty of time to play with the paint and spread it out or scribble in it. Encourage them to use both hands and all their fingers.
5. Try making some prints by covering the paint with paper, gently smoothing it down and peeling it off.

another idea:
* Make some hand or finger prints on paper or in the paint.

Ready for more?

* Stick black paper on a table and offer white or yellow paint for hand printing.
* Use a stamp pad (with washable ink!) to make finger prints.
* Go outside & make footprints in mud or sand.

Individual needs

☼ Using both hands is difficult for some children. Help them by modelling what to do - encouraging and praising any effort.

☼ Allow plenty of time for children to get used to the activity alone before working with two or more children.

Safety Tip

✳ Put some moisturiser in the paint to stop it staining skin.

Watch, listen, reflect

👁 Look at the children's hands and fingers. Are they able to separate their index finger to make marks and patterns?

👁 Watch how the children work together. Do they look at each other's patterns and paintings?

👁 Listen for words and simple phrases used while they work.

Working together

Parents could:

* try finger painting at home.
* praise their children's efforts, even though there is no real 'picture'.

Practitioners could:

* encourage parents to come in and look at displays of the work children have done.
* discuss in the team all the activities they can plan which encourage the use of both hands.

Make your mark

Early marks and writing

What are they learning?

are they
  exploring how
  paint behaves?
  trying things out?
  enjoying it?
  using fingers?
this leads to
  * experimenting
  * more mark
  making

Movers, shakers and players

Aspect:
A Competent Learner

Components:
Representing

A Basket of Markers
experimenting with markers and marks

What you need
* a box or basket of all different sorts of marker pens, crayons and coloured pencils
* large sheets of paper
* sticky tape

What you do
This activity is suitable for groups of children. It's better if they stand up.
1. Cover a big table top with paper, and tape it down.
2. Put the markers in one or more shallow containers on the table.
3. Talk to the children about the different markers and show them some of the range on offer.
4. Stay near as the children begin to make marks with the markers on the big paper surface. Talk with them as they work, using colour, size and shape words - 'wiggly lines', 'thick blue stripes', 'little circles' etc.

another idea:
* Try this outside on the back of a very long piece of wallpaper along a path or patio. Anchor it with bricks.

Ready for more?
🖐 Try dripping some water on the finished marks and watch what happens.
🖐 Make a game of finding the right tops for the pens - 'big top, big pen, 'tiny top for a tiny pen.

Individual needs

○ Don't forget to give everyone a choice of markers. some children may only be able to choose from two, but they do need regular choices!
○ Taking off and putting on pen tops is a fine motor activity in itself. Make time for this in your planning.

Safety Tip

✳ Rolls of lining paper are very cheap - get them from DIY shops.

Watch, listen, reflect

👁 Watch the way children manipulate the markers and how they use them.
👁 Observe how their grip is developing from a palmar or fist grip to a more 'orthodox' finger and thumb grip.
👁 Listen to the conversations and note new words and phrases.

Working together

Parents could:

* provide pens and paper frequently for their children.
* make sure their children see them writing. This will provide a good reason for the children to become writers and mark makers.

Practitioners could:

* talk to the parents about the importance of free access to mark making materials at home.
* make sure the children see adults writing for real purposes - making notes, labels and other writing in the setting. Models are important!

Make your mark

Early marks and writing

What are they learning?

are they
    holding and
    gripping?
    enjoying making
    marks?
    concentrating?
    looking?
this leads to
    * becoming a
      writer
    * using tools

Make your mark

Early marks and writing

Movers, shakers and players

Aspect:
A Competent Learner

Components:
Representing

Spray It
hand control out of doors

What you need

* small spray bottles (get ones that are easy to squeeze and check the trigger is not too far away for small hands to grip)
* thin paint or food colouring and water; paper or fabric

What you do

Activity suitable for a small group on a fine day!

1. Pin up some paper or fabric on a fence or other vertical surface (you could peg an old sheet over a washing line).
2. Fill the spray bottles with thin paint or water and food colouring.
3. Explain to the children that the sprays are for painting.
4. Show them how they work and where they may spray to make a spraying, drippy, runny picture.

Note: Keep the same sheet of paper or fabric up all day so lots of children can have a go - the resulting spray picture will make a wonderful hanging for your setting

another idea:
* Use the sprays to wash the wheeled toys.

Ready for more?

* Paint a simple picture on a wall and use sprays of water to wash it off.
* Use sprays to water plants, wash windows, or to make wrapping paper or wallpaper for your role play corner.

Individual needs

✿ Children with poor grip may need a lot of help from you in this activity, but it's such good fun, it's worth getting a bit wet!

✿ Try holding a piece of absorbent paper such as a paper towel in front of the spray to get a good close up effect.

Tiny Tip

❋ Try DIY stores or garden centres for indoor plant sprays, they are usually smaller.

Watch, listen, reflect

👁 Look at how each child grips and aims their spray. Can they do both at once?

👁 Note any children who look closely at what is happening to the paint on the paper or fabric.

👁 Listen to the words and phrases the children use as they work. Who can talk and work at the same time?

Working together

Parents could:

★ borrow a spray from your setting and play with it at home (in the garden or bath).

★ have fun with their children in simple play activities.

Practitioners could:

★ add some small spray bottles to the loan collection.

★ invite parents in to see the results of the children's work with sprays. Take some photos to display too.

Make your mark

Early marks and writing

What are they learning?

are they
　having fun?
　following rules?
　using hands'?
　aware of others?
this leads to
　* creativity
　* group work
　* understanding rules

121

Movers, shakers and players

Aspect:
A Competent Learner

Components:
Being creative

Messy Together
getting creative together

What you need

* large pieces of sponge foam and bubble wrap
* sticky tape and scissors
* bubble liquid
* gentle bubble bath in a small amount of warm water

What you do

This activity is suitable for groups of two to four children.

1. Spread the foam and bubble wrap out on the floor next to each other and tape down securely.
2. Pour the bubble bath mixture onto the foam and bubble wrap. Remove all unnecessary clothing and enjoy patting, crawling on and stamping on the bubbly mats.
3. Blow bubbles for the children to pop and stamp on as they land on the mats.
4. Sing simple commentaries, such as 'This is the way we pop the bubbles, pop the bubbles, pop the bubbles...', or 'The hands on the mat go pat, pat, pat...'

another idea:

* Tape down a foil survival blanket, (available from camping shops) and try the bubbles on a reflective surface.

Ready for more?

* Fill small buckets with warm bubbly water and let the children paint on the mats with large brushes, or washing up brushes and sponges.
* Pull on waterproofs and wellies and do it outside, best on a windy day!

122

Individual needs

☼ Watch out for allergies and children with sensitive skin or eczema. Talk to parents before you try the activity.

☼ This is a great activity for children with autistic spectrum disorders. Start by copying their actions, then gradually encourage them to imitate your actions and take turns.

Tiny tip

✳ Make sure children don't run over the soapy mats – they will be slippery!

Watch, listen, reflect

👁 Note the range of ways in which the child is exploring the different surfaces and the bubbles.

👁 Listen for describing words as well as single words and short phrases. Listen for spontaneous language.

👁 Watch how the children interact with each other and with adults, both verbally and non-verbally.

Working together

Parents could:

* borrow a 'pat mat' from their local toy library, or give their child sponges and flannels to play with at bath time.

* put together a basket of pieces of different coloured and textured fabrics for their child to explore and play with.

Practitioners could:

* review the range of creative activities they provide for indoor and outdoor play.

* talk to parents about the importance of creative activities for very young children and the range of play provided within the setting.

Let's explore

Exploring and creating

What are they learning?

are they
  sharing fun?
  turn taking?
  using whole body to explore?
  trying out new materials?
this leads to
  *small group play
  *pretend play
  *creativity

Movers, shakers and players

Aspect:
A Competent Learner

Components:
Being creative

124

Messy Stretchy
more creative fun together

What you need

* a large sheet of paper
* sticky tape and scissors
* sponges
* small balls with holes in, or balloons
* narrow elastic, trays of paint

What you do

Activity suitable for a small group.

1. Tape the large sheet of paper to the wall. Fix short lengths of elastic to the partially inflated balloons or small balls. Pierce the sponges with the scissors, thread the elastic through the holes and tie securely.
2. Let each child hold an elastic with ball, sponge or balloon attached and dip it in trays of paint.
3. Take turns to swing, stretch and ping the elastic, splatting the sponges, balls and balloons onto the paper.
4. Talk about the different patterns, colours and shapes created.

another idea:

* Tape a length of old wallpaper to the floor and try trailing the balls, sponges, balloons along the length of the paper.

Ready for more?

🖐 Fix lengths of elastic with tape at both ends across a tray. Slip paper underneath and dribble runny paint on top. Experiment with pinging the elastic.

🖐 Scrunch up small pieces of paper, bubble wrap etc. for printing.

Individual needs

✿ Some children will prefer to work on their own creation. Give them choices.

✿ Fix simple handles to the ends of the string, perhaps a plastic bangle or spoon, to give children with fine motor difficulties an easier grip.

✿ Encourage turn taking and 'Ready steady go' for added communication.

Tiny Tip

✳ Make sure the parents' entrance has lots of information about what you are doing to help the children be creative.

Watch, listen, reflect

👁 Look at the way the children are working together. Are they able to take turns, share ideas and imitate actions?

👁 Listen to the way they use language with each other and with adults.

👁 Watch how they investigate the elastic and the paint and try out new ideas.

Working together

Parents could:

* play alongside their children tearing and sticking pictures from magazine onto old envelopes.
* try 'painting' outside with soapy water, old paintbrushes, feathers, twigs and so on.

Practitioners could:

* make sure children have plenty of uninterrupted and unhurried time to explore creative activities.
* plan activities that do not have an end result but are creative opportunities offered during the activity.

Let's explore

Exploring and creating

What are they learning?

are they
turn taking?
exploring?
shared fun?
working together?
making marks?
this leads to
* finding out about colour, shape & pattern
* exploring

Movers, shakers
and players

Aspect:
A Competent
Learner

Components:
Being creative

Kaleidoscope Colours
changing-colour treasure basket

What you need
* a basket of multi-coloured objects,
  transparent coloured paper,
  textured coloured fabrics,
  coloured netting, multi-coloured
  gloves, kaleidoscopes, coloured
  viewers, coloured transparent
  shapes, coloured plastic bottles
* a white sheet or rug

What you do

This activity is suitable for pairs and small groups.
1. Spread the sheet or rug on the floor and place the basket
   of coloured objects and materials on the rug.
2. Sit with the children, exploring the different objects,
   talking about them, feeling them on different parts of
   the body, peeking through them and so on.
3. Try layering the transparent objects, and looking at the
   changing colours and patterns.
4. Encourage the children to use short phrases, describing
   words, both echoed and spontaneously, to comment on
   their play.

another idea:
* Try a treasure basket of silver and gold coloured objects
  and materials.

Ready for more?
🖐 Try shining coloured
   torches through
   coloured cellophane on
   the white sheet.
🖐 Play with coloured
   water and clear and
   coloured plastic
   bottles. Try a tube and
   funnel fixed to a wall
   outside.

Individual needs

✿ Try different coloured and textured plastic bangles and scrunchies on the hands and wrists of children at a very early developmental stage.
✿ Make sure children with visual difficulties sit in a good light, and are allowed plenty of exploring time.

Tiny Tip

❉ Make simple fabric lids for the treasure baskets. Add a slit in the middle for 'feely box' play.

Watch, listen, reflect

👁 Watch how the children use their senses to explore the objects and materials.
👁 Are they keen to share their discoveries?
👁 Listen to the language used and note the purposes of language.
👁 Listen for comparisons with their own life and surroundings, such as 'like Mummy's', or perhaps 'same'.

Working together

Parents could:

* talk to their child as they are out and about, describing what they see. Talk about colours and patterns.
* add lots of coloured toys to bath time play, and practise finding the same colour.

Practitioners could:

* make a list of objects needed for the treasure baskets and ask parents to help.
* make a display about treasure basket play, including example treasure baskets, photos of children playing and some ideas for baskets.

Let's explore

Exploring and creating

What are they learning?

are they
   exploring colour?
   using senses?
   describing words?
   sharing fun?
this leads to
   * exploring and investigating
   * creativity
   * describing, questioning

Let's explore

Exploring and creating

Movers, shakers and players

Aspect:
A Competent Learner

Components:
Being creative

128

Squidge It!
messy mark making

What you need

* bath crayons
* nail brushes
* sponges
* plastic trays or tin lids

What you do

This activity is suitable for groups of children.

1. Dampen the trays or tin lids. Play alongside the children with the bath crayons, encouraging mark making.
2. Help the children to focus on what they are doing and stay on task by commenting on what they are doing.
3. Add the sponges and the nail brushes to try different effects on the colour applied to the trays and tin lids.
4. Play at making circular patterns as well as up-and-down, and side-to-side marks.
5. Allow the children plenty of time and freedom to experiment with the mark making.

another idea:

* Tape a large sheet of clear plastic to a wall and play with the bath crayons, encouraging whole arm movements.

Ready for more?

* Try mark making outside with ribbon and string trailed through pools of water and then traced along the paths.
* Throw sponges full of water onto the ground outside to make lots of different splats.

Individual needs

☼ Look for chunky easy-to-grip bath crayons for children with fine motor difficulties or particularly small hands.

☼ Encourage all children to use two hands, one to make marks and the second to hold the tray still.

☼ Use washable felt pens for children who cannot apply sufficient pressure.

Tiny Tip

✳ Put together a basket of old envelopes, pens and parcels, used birthday cards, brochures and postcards.

Watch, listen, reflect

👁 Look at the way children are holding the crayons. What sort of grip do they prefer? Do they have an emerging hand preference?

👁 Can the children do circular scribble? Are they able to copy vertical and horizontal lines?

👁 Look out for early attempts at faces or people.

Working together

Parents could:

* play alongside their child, scribbling and mark making together.
* create a special place at home to display their child's pictures.

Practitioners could:

* make a list of all the early mark making activities they are providing for children, for parents to see.
* offer a mark-making workshop for parents and children, with lots of different mark-making activities and ideas.

Let's explore

Exploring and creating

What are they learning?

are they
   mark making?
   fine motor skills?
   attending?
this leads to
   * more mark making
   * writing/drawing
   * creativity
   * early literacy

Resources for all stages of A Competent Learner

Bargain buys for mark making

Try Pound Shops and other bargain outlets for
* paintbrushes and other decorator's tools
* sponges and brushes
* plastic sheets and shower curtains
* bargain felt pens
* funnels, tubes and sieves
* containers and pots

Try DIY stores for
* paint brushes
* sand and gravel
* dust sheets
* rollers, sponge rollers
* plant saucers & trays
* builders trays

Try Charity Shops for
* kitchen tools
* old shirts for painting
* curtains for dust sheets
* containers for equipment
* baskets for treasures
* trays and tins

Always wash or sterilise things before use.

Resources

Builder's Trays and plant trays
Get these from DIY stores

Feely Bags
NES Arnold, Galt, Early Learning

Textured balls
ASCO Educational Supplies (they also supply sensory tiles and sand boxes)
tel: 0113 270 7070

Gloop

Mix cornflour with water (and colouring if you want). The gloop should have a thick consistency - add extra water if necessary.

Bubble Solution

Make your own bubble solution from 2 cups (500ml) washing up liquid, 6 cups (1.5L) water and 5 tablespoons sugar. Store in an empty gallon container. Buy the best quality washing up liquid yo can afford, or use bubble bath.

Finger paint

Make finger paint by mixing two tablespoons of cornflour and two tablespoons of cold water in a saucepan. Add 1 cup of water an cook till it is as thick as custard (stirring all the time). Store in the fridge. Colour with paint or food colouring, and add perfumed oils to make it smell good.

Slime

Dissolve some Lux soap flakes in war water in a container. Add colouring, desired. Allow mixture to stand unt it becomes thick, add more water if necessary. Beat the mixture with eg beaters until fluffy.

Songs and rhymes

These songs and rhymes are suitable for developing hands, fingers, feet and fine motor skills. They are all in This Little Puffin (Penguin Books) or in The Little Book of Nursery Rhymes (Featherstone Education)

Finger songs and rhymes

Five Little Peas
Heads, Shoulders, Knees and Toes
Here are the Lady's Knives & Forks
Here is a Box
Here's The Church and Here's the Steeple
Incy Wincy Spider
My Little House
One Finger, One Thumb Keep Moving
One Potato, Two Potato
Pat-a-Cake, Pat-a-Cake
Peter Hammers with One Hammer
Roly, Poly Up and Down
Round and Round the Garden
She Didn't Dance
Teddy Bear, Teddy Bear
This Little Pig Went to Market
Tommy Thumb
Two Little Dicky Birds
Wind the Bobbin
Songs to help imitation & imagination
Daddy's Taking us to the Zoo

Dingle Dangle Scarecrow
Five Currant Buns
Five Little Ducks
Five Little Men in a Flying Saucer
Five Little Monkeys
Heads, Shoulders, Knees and Toes
Here is The Beehive
Here we go Round the Mulberry Bush
Hokey Kokey
I am the Music Man
If You're Happy and You Know It
I'm a Little Teapot
In a Cottage in a Wood
In a Dark, Dark Wood
Insy Winsy Spider
I Went to Visit a Farm one day
Little Peter Rabbit
Little Rabbit FouFou
Miss Polly had a Dolly
Old MacDonald had a Farm
1, 2, 3, 4, 5 Once I Caught a Fish Alive
1 Finger, 1 Thumb Keep Moving

Pat a Cake
Peter Hammers with One Hammer
Roly Poly
Round and Round the Village
Row, Row, Row Your Boat
Sandy Girl
Teddy Bear, Teddy Bear, Touch Your Nose
The Farmer's in His Den
The Wheels on the Bus
There was a Princess Long Ago
This is the Way the Lady Rides
This Old Man, He Played One
Tommy Thumb
Twinkle, Twinkle, Little Star
Two Fat Gentlemen
Two Little Dickey Birds
We Can Play on the Big Bass Drum
When Goldilocks Went
When I was One
Wind the Bobbin up

Books about Treasure Baskets

Title	Author	Publisher
* <u>Infants at Work</u>	Elinor Goldschmied	NCB (1987)
* <u>People Under Three</u>	Elinor Goldschmied& Sonia Jackson	Routledge
* <u>The Little Book of Treasure Baskets</u>	Ann Roberts	Featherstone Education

Movers,
Shakers
and
Players

Aspect and
components

Section 4

The Following section contains activities for young children, to help build **a Healthy Child**

The relevant Birth to Three Matters components are:
* **Growing and Developing**
* **Keeping Safe**
* **Making Healthy Choices**
* **Emotional Wellbeing**

Movers, shakers and players

Aspect:
A Healthy Child

Components:
Growing and developing

134

First Fingers
index finger fun

What you need
* small plastic cups and plates
* cooked noodles
* jelly
* yoghurt
* bread

What you do

1. Spread a tiny drop of runny yoghurt on to a plastic plate or tray. Stuff bits of bread and pasta in the cups.
2. Put a tiny drop of runny yoghurt on the baby's and your own index fingers. Trail your index fingers around the plate, making patterns and swirls. Stop and place your index fingers on the child's index fingers. Play at tapping the sticky fingers together. Add more yoghurt to index fingers and enjoy sliding fingers back and forth and round and round in the goo.
3. Play at poking and prodding index fingers into the plastic cups. Take turns with the child to prod and poke. Feel the different shapes and textures.

another idea:
* Try poking holes in pizza or bread dough.

Ready for more?
🖐 Play 'Round and round the garden', taking turns to use the first finger to show Teddy going round and round the garden.
🖐 Use a toy keyboard. Encourage each child to play first with index fingers and then to use each finger separately.

Individual needs

○ Remember that some children may be really sensitive on their hands and intensely dislike some textures and consistencies.

○ Some children may need lots of very simple individual finger play, such as tapping fingers, pointing and prodding, to help them isolate their index finger.

Tiny Tip

✻ Check out The Little Book of Nursery Rhymes and This Little Puffin for a comprehensive collection of traditional finger rhymes.

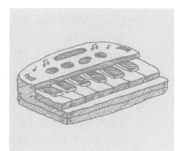

Watch, listen, reflect

👁 Watch out for emerging hand preference. Look carefully at the way children pick up objects, how they use their fingers and thumbs.

👁 Observe how children use a pointing gesture to support their first words.

👁 Listen to and encourage children to combine words, pointing and gesture.

Working together

Parents could:

* tell practitioners their child's favourite rhymes.
* allow for messy food play and finger feeding at mealtimes.
* find out why finger play is so important.

Practitioners could:

* get together with colleagues and make a list of all the finger rhymes they know, and share these with parents and the children regularly.
* make time every day to share a finger rhyme individually with their key children.

Grab - and let go

Developing fine motor skills

What are they learning?

are they
  isolating index fingers?
  using fingers and thumbs together?
  exploring?
  trying new things?
  making sounds?
this leads to
  * pincer grip
  * pencil control

Developing fine
motor skills

Movers, shakers
and players

Aspect:
A Healthy Child

Components:
Growing and
developing

Clap Hands!
feathers and streamers

What you need

* feathers (available from craft or needlework shops)
* ribbons
* chiffon scarves

What you do

1. Blow the feathers into the air for the children to touch. Start by touching them with isolated index fingers and then try clapping to catch the feathers. Sing 'Everybody do this, do this, just like me.'
2. Drop the chiffon scarves from high up and see if the children can clap hands to catch them. Blow them into the air and clap to catch them as they fall.
3. Next, tie ribbons into bundles that will slip gently over the children's wrists. Clap hands together to favourite nursery rhymes, such as 'Baa, Baa, Black Sheep', or 'Jack and Jill'.

another idea:
* Blow bubbles. Pop by clapping hands together.

Ready for more?

* Sing 'Wind the bobbin up' and 'Roly, Poly, Poly' (both in 'This Little Puffin') and practise rolling arms action.
* Take time when washing hands to clap and slide soapy hands together.

Individual needs

☼ Make sure children are sitting straight and if on a chair, have their feet firmly on the ground.

☼ Help children who clap to show their excitement, to use a new word or gesture to make a specific request, eg if they clap excitedly when they see the juice, smile, point to the cup and say, 'Drink'.

Tiny Tip

✳ Don't push children to join in with action rhymes and clapping games. Make it fun. They will join in when they are ready.

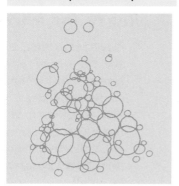

Watch, listen, reflect

👁 Look at the range of different gestures and actions the children are using.

👁 Listen, copy and praise any sounds they make.

👁 Observe what interests each child and helps to hold their attention on an activity or song.

Working together

Parents could:

* share a nursery song and rhyme book with their child.
* make a nursery song part of bedtime routine.

Practitioners could:

* lend nursery rhyme tapes and books to parents.
* give parents the words and movements to their child's favourite action rhymes.

Grab - and let go

Developing fine motor skills

What are they learning?

are they
    using 2 hands?
    copying actions?
    looking?
    listening?
    making sounds?
    co-ordinating
    hands and eyes?
this leads to
    * fine motor skill
    * mark making

Developing fine
motor skills

Movers, shakers
and players

Aspect:
A Healthy Child

Components:
Growing and
developing

138

Thank You
offering objects in tower play

What you need

* stacking bricks
* small basket

What you do

1. Build a tower of the bricks and invite the child to come and play. Watch them knock it down! Try to help them wait with a 'Ready, steady', then pause 'Go'.
2. Place all the bricks in the basket. Give them the basket and ask them to pass you a brick. Stretch out your hand. Start to build a tower. Ask the child to pass each brick into your outstretched hand. If they want to help build the tower, take it in turns to pass each other a brick. When the tower is complete, do 'Ready steady go' again, encouraging the child to wait for 'Go'.
3. Gather all the bricks together and play again.

another idea:
* Try stacking shoeboxes, or create a very wobbly tower with a selection of junk modelling boxes.

Ready for more?

🖐 Play tea parties, asking the child to offer tiny bits of fruit or bread to other children.
🖐 Play together in the home corner, asking the child to bring you different objects, such as a doll.

Individual needs

☼ Make passing objects into an outstretched hand an important and practical step towards independence of children.

☼ For children needing more help to understand the outstretched hand gesture, ask another adult to gently help the child reach out towards your hand.

Tiny Tip

✻ A gentle tickle on the back of the hand will help reluctant fingers to open!

Watch, listen, reflect

👁 Observe the different natural gestures that each child uses. Think about how much they rely on these gestures and which expressions and phrases they understand without these gesture clues.

👁 Look at the child's body language – are they enjoying sharing and receiving praise?

👁 Listen & note the words they use.

Working together

Parents could:

* encourage their child to pass them items of clothing as they help them to get dressed.
* ask children to choose and pass their bedtime storybook.

Practitioners could:

* think of practical ways to encourage each child's independence.
* practise passing Teddy round a small circle of three or four children.

Grab - and let go

What are they learning?

are they
    anticipating?
    sharing?
    turn taking?
    releasing
    objects?
    reaching out?
this leads to
    * co-operative
       play
    * communication

Movers, shakers and players

Aspect:
A Healthy Child

Components:
Growing and developing

140

Fingers and Thumbs
stickers and stars

What you need

* pens
* small sticky labels
* star stickers

What you do

1. Place a star sticker on each child's and your own index fingers.
2. Sing 'Twinkle Twinkle Little Star' together, pointing index fingers to the sky.
3. Place a star sticker on every finger and thumb, and sing the rhyme again.
4. Help the children to draw a small circle on two plain sticky labels, and add legs to make a spider. Place the spider stickers on the pads of the thumbs. Sing 'Incy, Wincy Spider' with the actions, bringing fingers and thumbs together as the spider climbs the spout.

another idea:
* Draw bird shapes on two stickers and sing the 'Two Little Dickey Birds' rhyme.

Ready for more?

🖐 Collect some old bracelets and necklaces and play at putting these on each other and soft toys.
🖐 Provide a bowl of cooked noodles for some fun finger play.

Individual needs

☼ Use reflective or fluorescent colours for the stickers for children with visual difficulties.

☼ Place a smiley face sticker on the palm of your hand to encourage reluctant children to get involved with this activity.

☼ Keep the activity very short and focused.

Tiny Tip

✳ Bubbles are brilliant for helping children to isolate their index finger and reach accurately.

Watch, listen, reflect

👁 Observe what motivates the children. What can you do to help them maintain their attention on the activity?

👁 Note the range of gestures used and if children are able to imitate the actions in the rhymes.

👁 Listen for single and two word phrases. Decide if the words used are all object words.

Working together

Parents could:

★ try out the star stickers and twinkle twinkle game at home.

★ put together a treasure basket of small but safe objects for their child to explore at home.

Practitioners could:

★ enlist the help of parents and volunteers in making finger puppets.

★ collect suitable objects for a fingers and thumbs treasure basket.

Grab - and let go

Developing fine motor skills

What are they learning?

are they
    playing together?
    imitating?
    using fingers and
    thumbs?
    using new words?

this leads to
    * shared attention
    * pencil grip

Movers, shakers and players

Aspect:
A Healthy Child

Components:
Growing and developing

142

In My Hand
using brushes and sponges

What you need

* lots of different brushes and sponges (washing up brush or sponge, nail brush, tooth brush, paint brush, cotton buds)
* paint, paint tray, big paper

What you do

1. Tape the paper to the floor. Mix the paint and place in shallow trays with the brushes.
2. Allow plenty of time and freedom for the children to try out the different brushes and experiment with how they can hold and use the brushes.
3. Play alongside the children. Observe the way they are holding the different brushes. Look out for circular movements and also for large up and down paint strokes.
4. Use simple short phrases to describe what they are doing such as 'Pat, pat, pat' or 'Up and down'.

another idea:
* Use large decorators' paintbrushes and a bowl of soapy water outside for painting on the ground and walls.

Ready for more?

* Try painting with big brushes on large cardboard boxes outside. Paint rollers work well and need a different sort of grip and action.
* Dip lengths of ribbon and string in water and make trails outside.

Individual needs

○ Play alongside children who need encouragement. Allow plenty of time for them to watch and perhaps share painting with you.

○ Give their own paper and paints to children who prefer to work in their own space.

Tiny Tip

❋ Some children will instinctively take a toothbrush to their mouth! Take care, it could be loaded with paint!!

Watch, listen, reflect

◉ Watch how the children grip the brushes and sponges. Look for whole hand palmar grips and finger and thumb pincer grips.

◉ Look at the shapes and movements they are making.

◉ Think about the different ways they are experimenting and finding out about using tools.

Working together

Parents could:

★ let children paint with water in the garden.

★ try wet chalks at home.

Practitioners could:

★ make painting and mark making a part of every-day experiences inside and out.

★ make a list for parents of the sorts of resources they want them to collect, such as decorators' brushes, craft tools and so on.

Grab - and let go

Developing fine motor skills

What are they learning?

are they
 exploring?
 holding?
 using wrist and hand?
 watching?
 responding?

this leads to
 ★ hand control
 ★ use of tools

Tickle and tumble

Feeling safe and supported

Movers, shakers and players

Aspect:
A Healthy Child

Components:
Keeping safe

Choose
first choices, first risks

What you need

* small bowls
* 3 or 4 different colours of finger paint
* table top, plastic sheet or board screwed to the wall

What you do

Children will need protective clothing for this activity, which support decision making and choice.
1. Put some finger paint in the bowls.
2. Protect the children's clothes and explain where they can paint and that they can choose their own colours.
3. Offer them the whole range of colours and let them choose which they use.
4. Stay with the activity, but try not to interfere! This activity is about independence and choice, so use the opportunity to observe how the children make choices.
5. Only intervene when the children lose interest.

another idea:
* Try putting sand or glitter in some of the colours to make the choice more interesting.

Ready for more?

☝ Offer a range of different materials for a free choice sticking activity.
☝ Encourage the children to choose books for story time as early and as often as possible.

Individual needs

☼ Children with restricted movement sometimes have fewer opportunities to choose for themselves. Make sure you remember to give them real choices whenever you can. Encourage eye pointing, finger pointing, gesture and sounds, and hold objects, drinks, snacks, toys and activities where they can see to choose.

Tiny Tip

✳ Make sure the choices are genuine - watch yourself to eliminate body movements or expressions that may affect children's choices.

Watch, listen, reflect

👁 Watch for emerging independence in choice.

👁 Listen to the way some children talk themselves through the choice making process.

👁 Watch for children who make multiple choices and those who appear not to be able to choose at all without support from you. They need plenty more practice!

Working together

Parents could:

* offer their children appropriate choices at home.
* tell practitioners about children's growing ability to choose independently.

Practitioners could:

* make choice and independence firm principles in your policy and practice. Make sure parents understand that this is an important part of growing up.
* build choice into everyday routines.

Tickle and tumble

Feeling safe and supported

What are they learning?

are they
    choosing for
    themselves?
    showing
    confidence?
    exploring?
    trying new things?
this leads to
    * independence
    * further choice

Movers, shakers and players

Aspect:
A Healthy Child

Components:
Keeping safe

146

Goodnight Teddy
caring for a toy

What you need

* dressed doll
* night clothes
* doll's bed or shoe box
* covers or pieces of fabric for blankets

What you do

This activity is suitable for one, two or three children.

1. Tell the children that the doll is poorly and needs to be looked after. Talk about what the children could do to look after him/her.
2. Follow the children's ideas, they may want to give the doll medicine (from a 'real' or pretend spoon and bottle); they may want to take her/him to the doctor.
3. Talk about what happens to them when they are poorly. Who looks after them, what they do. Do they go to bed, lie on the settee, stay with Grandma?
4. Use the objects you have prepared or collect more with the children.

another idea:
* Add a white shirt and a badge for a doctor or nurse.

Ready for more?

- Sing 'Miss Polly had a Dolly', (in This Little Puffin) and practise the actions.
- Find some books and stories about children who are ill.

Individual needs

☼ Use small world people and small boxes with very small pieces of fabric for children who are restricted to chairs or buggies.

☼ Listen carefully to their experiences and ideas about illness and being looked after.

Tiny Tip

✲ Ask the local Health Visitor to visit to talk about being poorly and visiting the doctor.

Watch, listen, reflect

👁 Watch for care and concern in words and actions.

👁 Look for any copying of models of familiar adults.

👁 Note the differences between the children's experiences of being ill and being looked after.

Working together

Parents could:

* tell practitioners what happens to their child when they are poorly.
* play the 'being poorly' game with their children.

Practitioners could:

* add books about families and caring to the toy library.
* be clear about what will happen if the children become unwell at your setting.

Tickle and tumble

Feeling safe and supported

What are they learning?

are they
    taking care?
    sympathising?
    remembering
    describing?
    talking?

this leads to
    * empathy
    * sequencing
    * imagining
    * making stories

147

Tickle and tumble

Feeling safe and supported

Movers, shakers and players

Aspect:
A Healthy Child

Components:
Keeping safe

148

Snack Time
making choices in snack time

What you need

* beakers/cups (different colours)
* small and serving plates
* at least two different juices or drinks
* a selection of fruit, raw vegetables, raisins, crackers

What you do

Use this activity to build on something you already do in your setting. Concentrate on making choices, trying new things and talking about likes and dislikes.

1. Let the children help with the preparation of the drinks and snacks, and the table where you will sit.
2. Put one type of snack on each serving plate to make the choices clear. Put the drinks in jugs, or leave them in their bottles/boxes so children can see the different fruits.
3. During the snack session, concentrate on helping the children to make choices by asking each in turn to choose their plate, mug, drink and snack.

another idea:
* Liven up snack time by having a picnic, or by eating outside or in the home corner.

Ready for more?

🖐 Have a tea party and give the children choices of food and drinks (real or pretend).
🖐 Give children choices of food at lunchtime, if you can.

Individual needs

✿ Young children find choice very difficult - limit choice to two things until they are more confident.

✿ All children should be given choices from the youngest age. Some need to gesture, touch, point or eye point, so make sure the objects are near enough and far enough apart to see their preferences.

Tiny Tip

✳ Try using low sugar fruit squashes and let them add their own water from small plastic jugs.

Watch, listen, reflect

👁 Watch for children who can't make choices. Perhaps the range is too wide - if so, stick to two things.

👁 Note whether children are confident enough to choose or follow the last child's choice.

👁 Make sure you present the choices evenly, so you don't influence their choice to meet your expectations!

Working together

Parents could:

* give their children simple choices at home, and give a choice between two things, not hundreds! Too much choice makes children feel insecure.

* understand that choice is part of growing up.

Practitioners could:

* explain why choice is an important part of growing up, and isn't about letting children have their own way all the time!

* give children choices when they can.

Tickle and tumble

Feeling safe and supported

What are they learning?

are they
   watching?
   choosing?
   seeing
   differences?
   talking?

this leads to
   * ability to choose
   * developing likes & dislikes

Tickle and tumble

Feeling safe and supported

Movers, shakers and players

Aspect:
A Healthy Child

Components:
Keeping safe

150

Family Fun
talking about relationships

What you need

* baby dolls
* baby clothes, nappies, bottles, comforters
* blankets, pram, pushchair

What you do

1. Sit with one or two children - maybe in the home corner.
2. Hold one of the baby dolls in your arms as if it was a real baby. Talk to the baby and the children about how you are the mum or dad, and this is your baby. Invite them to join you with a baby of their own.
3. Start to role play being a parent - talk about the baby being tired, hungry or needing to be changed. Encourage the children to talk about their babies. Help them to talk about what parents and babies do together. Sing to the babies, change them, take them for a walk.
4. Emphasise the caring aspects of being a parent by talking about feelings of safety and security, holding and loving.

another idea:
* Ask a parent to bring their baby to visit your setting.

Ready for more?

✋ Join a group of children playing with small world animalss or people families. Talk about how different families keep their babies safe.
✋ Look at mother and baby books, human and animals.

Individual needs

☼ Try using a small size baby doll for children who have mobility or manipulative difficulties.

☼ Children with special needs are often so cared for themselves, they need the opportunity to learn the language and skills of caring for someone else.

Tiny Tip

✳ Make sure boys also have frequent opportunities for involvement in caring activities.

Watch, listen, reflect

👁 Watch and listen for the language children use in playing out their experiences of families.

👁 Observe how children hold and care for the dolls as they play.

👁 Look for children modelling the language and movements of caring for each other.

Working together

Parents could:

* talk about and demonstrate the caring aspects of families.
* make sure every family member - (boys and girls, mothers and fathers) get involved in all aspects of family life.

Practitioners could:

* put some baby dolls in the toy library.
* explain to parents the importance of children feeling secure and loved within their family, and the effect of this on confidence and learning.

Tickle and tumble

Feeling safe and supported

What are they learning?

are they
   taking care?
   modelling caring adults?
   using appropriate language?

this leads to
* confidence and self esteem
* understanding relationships

Tickle and tumble

Feeling safe and supported

Movers, shakers and players

Aspect:
A Healthy Child

Components:
Keeping safe

Everything in its Place
sorting and organising

What you need

* a basket of things collected from round your setting (small toys, crayons, pieces of construction, scrap paper, a paint brush, etc.)

What you do

Helping to clear up and organise their surroundings is a first responsibility for young children. The sooner they understand the organisation of your setting, the sooner they will feel a real part of it. Use this game to help them learn the proper places for things and have some fun doing it!

1. Collect together two or three children.
2. Tip the objects out of the basket onto the floor.
3. Look at each one and talk about where it belongs.
4. Let the children take turns to choose an object and take it to the place it belongs. Praise them when they get it right. If they can't find the place, help them by giving verbal clues.

another idea:
* Reverse the game and ask the children in turn to fetch items from around the room or garden.

Ready for more?

* Let the children help you make labels for equipment boxes and stick them on.
* Cut pictures from catalogues and use these to label equipment boxes, shelves, etc.

Individual needs

- All children need to be involved in tidying up after their own activities. Some will need more time and more help than others. Make sure you allow for this in your schedule and your planning.
- Some children are VERY unwilling to help clear up. They need plenty of praise for what they do.

Tiny Tip

❊ make sure children are involved with setting up and putting away activities - otherwise they think it happens by magic!

Watch, listen, reflect

- 👁 Watch how the children work as they are helping to clear up. Look for their sense of order and organisation.
- 👁 Note children who have difficulty finding where things go - give them help by talking them through the activity.
- 👁 Think about what they are learning in this activity.

Working together

Parents could:

- * help their children with clearing up at home, even though it takes longer than doing it themselves.
- * get some cheap plastic boxes or baskets to help their children get a sense of order and organisation.

Practitioners could:

- * explain why it is important for children to help with organisation.
- * show parents how you have made simple labels and organised things in your setting.

Tickle and tumble

Feeling safe and supported

What are they learning?

are they
  looking?
  using labels and
  pictures?
  helping each
  other?

this leads to
  * making sense
    of their
    environment
  * categorising

What can my body do?

Movers, shakers and players

Aspect:
A Healthy Child

Components:
Making healthy choices

154

Heavenly Hats
reaching, stretching, stopping, starting

What you need

* a collection of different hats - helmets, sun hats, rain hats, woolly hats, straw hats, caps
* a wall mirror, at an easily accessible height
* a tape or CD of dance music

What you do

Three children is about right for this activity.
1. Spread the hats out on the floor and give the children plenty of time to explore them, trying them on themselves and on you.
2. Place all the hats on the floor and get the children to stand around the edge.
3. Play the dance music. Dance together. When the music stops, each child chooses a hat.
4. Start the music again, dance and when the music stops, swap for a different hat!

another idea:
* Pass the hat around the group and when the music stops the child holding the hat puts it on. Choose another hat and play again. Keep going until all the children have a hat.

Ready for more?

☜ Wear hats and dance to music. When the music stops, nod the hat off! When it starts again, everyone grabs a hat and starts dancing again!
☜ See how many hats you can balance on your head and walk from one end of the room to the other!

Individual needs

☼ Make sure the hats are easy to pull on and off, floppy sun hats work well.

☼ Help easily excited children know the game is over, by taking turns to toss hats back into a box.

☼ Leave some hats in the home corner for shy children to try when they are ready.

Tiny Tip

❊ Charity shops have some great inexpensive hats, scarves and gloves at bargain prices! Try 'pound shops' for baseball caps and sun hats.

Watch, listen, reflect

👁 Look to see if children are watching each other.

👁 Watch to see if any of the children are anticipating you turning off the music.

👁 See how quickly the children pick up the rules of this simple game.

👁 Are the children making choices about which hat they want? Are they aware of the needs of others?

Working together

Parents could:

★ dance with their child!

★ ask amongst friends and family for old hats for your group.

Practitioners could:

★ make sure children can reach CDs and tapes, so they can ask for music to be played.

★ check that the dressing up clothes are attractive and in good repair.

★ fix a full-length mirror at child height.

Which one?

What can my body do?

What are they learning?

are they
   moving with
   confidence?
   listening?
   making choices?
   being part of a
   group?
this leads to
   ★ group play
   ★ listening skills
   ★ following rules

What can my body do?

Movers, shakers and players

Aspect:
A Healthy Child

Components:
Making healthy choices

In We Go!
still more choices

What you need

* a tunnel or indoor play tent
* old curtains or blankets
* net curtains or similar fabric
* a large cardboard box
* some soft toys

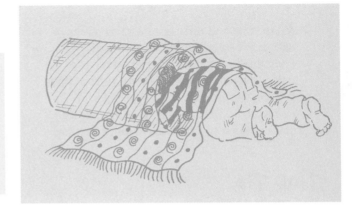

What you do

1. Open out the cardboard box at both ends to form a short tunnel. Cover the entrances of the box and the tunnel or indoor play tent with the old blankets, curtains or nets.
2. Ask the children to hide the soft toys in the tents.
3. Now play at finding different toys. Give the children plenty of choices, such as 'Should we find Teddy or Rabbit?'.
4. Be explorers and choose different entrances to the tunnels and tent.

another idea:
* Add some torches to take into the tunnels and tents.

Ready for more?

* Make some holes in the sides of the box for peeking in, or shining torches through.
* Fix some pictures or photos to the insides of the box, tunnel and play tent. Ask the children to hunt for named pictures.

Individual needs

✿ Make sure the tunnels and tents are on a soft surface suitable for children who are crawling or rolling.
✿ Use a transparent tunnel and net curtain for children needing more reassurance.
✿ Use just the play tent and offer just two choices for children at an early developmental stage.

Tiny Tip

❋ Take every opportunity to try out different ways of moving – giant strides to the milk table, slithering over to the coats and so on.

Watch, listen, reflect

👁 Look out for turn taking.
👁 Watch to see how children are relating to each other and for awareness of the needs of others.
👁 Think about the choices each child is making and why.
👁 Listen for action words as well as object words.

Working together

Parents could:

* encourage their child to try out different ways of moving.
* provide blankets and boxes for simple den building.

Practitioners could:

* think of all ways children can move and provide opportunities for children to experiment with movement.
* display information on local facilities for play and lists of local parks on the parent's notice board.

Which one?

What can my body do?

What are they learning?

are they
    moving with confidence?
    exploring?
    making choices?
    taking turns?
this leads to
    * group play
    * sharing and working together

Which one?

What can my body do?

Movers, shakers and players

Aspect:
A Healthy Child

Components:
Making healthy choices

Truly Sloppy!
cornflour and water play

What you need
* aprons!
* plastic bowls, jugs, wooden spoons
* plastic scrapers, tubes and tea strainers
* large shallow plastic tray

What you do
Children will need protective clothing for this activity, which support decision making and choice.
1. Cover everything and the children well!
2. Tip cornflour into the bowls and slowly add water.
3. Mix together using hands or wooden spoons.
4. Play with the cornflour mixture, tipping it into the shallow tray. Encourage the children to isolate their index finger to drizzle the mixture around, use two hands together to hold the bowls and stir, two hands together to pour and steady the jugs.
5. Rub sticky fingers together. Try rubbing the mixture in the flat of open palms, or between fingers and thumbs.

another idea:
* Add split peas or uncooked rice to the mixture.

Ready for more?
* Try mark making with fingers in a cornflour and water paste. Add brushes, corks, straws and rollers for more mark making in the goo.
* Coloured rice or split peas are great fun with tiny spoons and ice cube trays.

158

Individual needs

- ☼ Some children may dislike the feel of the cornflour and water mixture. Make sure you have lots of clean handled tools for them to use and a clean apron too!
- ☼ Encourage reluctant children to get involved by adding treasure to the mix – such as sequins or large buttons.
- ☼ Be aware of allergies and skin irritation.

Tiny Tip

❋ Tiny containers and spoons fascinate young children. Ice cube trays, clean fromage frais pots and tiny plastic boxes are ideal.

Watch, listen, reflect

- 👁 Watch for children isolating their index finger, using a pincer grip and so on. Can they use two hands together effectively?
- 👁 Listen for action words and describing words, and short phrases combining action and object words.
- 👁 Look to see how the children are trying out their own ideas, as well as copying the actions of others.

Working together

Parents could:

- ✱ give their child a small bowl of jelly to play with!
- ✱ make sure that their child has lots of opportunity to try mark making.

Practitioners could:

- ✱ make a recipe poster with play ideas – perhaps a simple play dough recipe, cornflour and water and so on.
- ✱ update the range of tools available for the children to use with malleable materials.

Which one?

What can my body do?

What are they learning?

are they
practising hand-eye co-ordination and different grips?
using two hands together?
trying new things?
this leads to
* sensory play
* motor control

Movers, shakers and players

Aspect:
A Healthy Child

Components:
Making healthy choices

160

Teddy and Company
what's for dinner?

What you need

* teddies and other soft toys
* small plastic bowls, spoons
* dried pasta, some pretend fruit and some pretend food such as sausages or pizza
* two small chairs or cushions

What you do

1. Sit a couple of soft toys on the chairs or cushions. Explain that they are really hungry. Rub their tummies and say 'Look, Teddy's feeling hungry'.
2. Invite each child to choose pasta or fruit for Teddy. Help them to fill a bowl and pretend to feed Teddy.
3. Play again, feeding the other toys. Use action words, object words and short phrases. Emphasise key words and phrases, such as 'all gone', 'hungry' and 'full'.
4. Talk to the children about mealtimes at home and in your setting. Ask about favourite foods.

another idea:
* Play this simple choice making game with soft toy animals, with clean pet food boxes, an empty milk carton to give the cat a drink, pretend lettuce and carrots for rabbits.

Ready for more?

🖐 Pass a box of play jewellery around a group of three children, taking turns to choose an item to put on. Pass a mirror round so each child can see how they look.
🖐 Make lots of different coloured paper planes. Take turns to choose a paper plane and fly it.

Individual needs

- ☼ Offer real choices between two familiar everyday objects to children with language delay.
- ☼ Give children with sensory difficulties plenty of time to explore the choices.
- ☼ Use visual clues such as objects, photos, or line drawings, as well as gestures to support understanding of choices.

Tiny Tip

✳ Take photos of every-day objects around your setting. Use the photos to support understanding and choice, and as visual clues.

Watch, listen, reflect

- 👁 Listen to how children express their choices. Are they aware of others, allowing time for them to make their choice?
- 👁 Note whether they are making genuine choices, or following other children or yourself?
- 👁 Watch to see if the children can take turns and maintain their attention when it is another's turn.

Working together

Parents could:

- ✶ offer real choices to their child at every opportunity.
- ✶ talk to their child as they are making their own choices.

Practitioners could:

- ✶ talk to parents about the importance of children making choices.
- ✶ look at drink and mealtime routines and consider how choice making can be extended for children at every stage.

Which one?

What can my body do?

What are they learning?

are they
  making choices?
  expressing their needs?
  using first words to describe feelings?
  taking turns?
this leads to
  ✶ turn taking
  ✶ following rules

Movers, shakers and players

Aspect:
A Healthy Child

Components:
Emotional wellbeing

Losing Teddy
a story about being lost

What you need

* an old teddy, doll or soft toy that the children will not recognise (get one from a charity shop and wash it first!)
* a simple card label, or an envelope with a letter inside

What you do

1. Tie the label round the toy's neck or leg, or write a letter to leave with it. Write:
   'I am lost and I can't find my home or my mummy. Please help me.'
2. Leave the bear or other toy in the garden or somewhere where the children will find it. (You may have to help!).
3. When you find him, ask the children what they think you should do. Follow their suggestions, and try not to influence their decisions.
4. Help them to do whatever they think they should do to help the lost toy.

another idea:
* Read some stories about being lost and ask the children how they felt if they were ever lost.

Ready for more?

* Sometimes leave a toy, a message or a lost item in the garden or setting for the children to talk about.
* Talk about things that make them feel safe and people who look after them.

Individual needs

☼ Make sure all children are involved in these activities. Try to make sure they can contribute to discussions and finding solutions.

☼ Children with communication difficulties need extra support and time to express feelings and fears.

Tiny Tip

✲ Be vigilant for children who find this activity stressful. Make sure you talk to them and reassure them that they are safe with you.

Watch, listen, reflect

👁 Watch for children who are anxious. Make time to talk to them.

👁 Listen for words and expressions of concern for others.

👁 Watch to make sure all the children are involved.

👁 Are the children thinking about how they could help the toy to find his way home? Do they have solutions?

Working together

Parents could:

* talk about scary situations with their child and reassure them that they are safe.
* teach their child what to do if they are lost. Help them to learn their telephone number.

Practitioners could:

* collect stories about emotions for the book corner and loan collection.
* teach children simple safety procedures. Help parents to understand that children need to explore scary feelings.

Me and you

Being together

What are they learning?

are they
    thinking about others?
    talking?
    suggesting solutions?
this leads to
    * problem solving
    * exploring and managing feelings

Movers, shakers and players

Aspect:
A Healthy Child

Components:
Emotional wellbeing

Fetch it For Me
go and come back

What you need
* a big sheet of fabric (eg. an old sheet, some lycra)
* a basket of objects to hide under the sheet (eg. soft toys, cars, a ball)
* two or three children

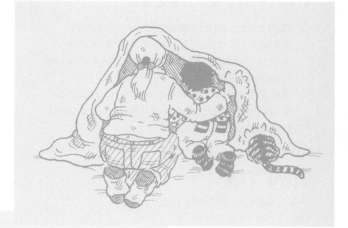

What you do
1. Spread the sheet on the carpet or grass.
2. Sit around the sheet, lift up the edge and peep underneath at the floor or grass.
3. Lift the edge of the sheet and put it over your heads to make a tent. Try to see right under the sheet to someone on the other side. Lay the sheet flat again.
4. Now show the children one of the toys, turn the sheet back and put the toy underneath. Pull the sheet back over the toy (don't put it too far under to start with).
5. Now ask 'Can you see where the teddy is? Who can go under the sheet and get him?'
6. Continue to play the game until the children have had a turn each. Don't force children to join in, let them just watch the others until they feel braver.

Ready for more?
🖐 Let children go under the sheet to put a toy there for someone else to fetch.
🖐 Play the same game with different fabrics to make different darknesses.
🖐 Take some torches under the sheets.

Individual needs

☼ Some children hate having their heads covered. Be sensitive and make sure you stay near for reassurance.

☼ Use a net curtain or open-weave fabric for children needing more reassurance.

☼ For children with limited mobility, put the toys just under the fabric and sit the child near the edge so they can reach out.

Tiny Tip

✳ Start with very small pieces of fabric, such as a scarf, and gradually increase the size until you are using a full sheet.

Watch, listen, reflect

👁 Watch for children who don't like having their heads or faces covered.

👁 Note the children who understand this game quickly and want more.

👁 Watch for attention and anticipation.

👁 Listen for action words and object words for the things they are looking for.

Working together

Parents could:

★ play this game when they are changing the sheets!

★ provide blankets and boxes for simple den building.

Practitioners could:

★ provide play sheets for loan to parents.

★ make a list of all the ways you can use a sheet or square of fabric. Put the list up for parents or make copies so they can take them home.

Me and you

Being together

What are they learning?

are they
   moving with confidence?
   exploring?
   enjoying the fun?
   watching others?
this leads to
   * confidence
   * playing games
   * object permanence

Movers, shakers and players

Aspect:
A Healthy Child

Components:
Emotional wellbeing

Inside
in a box

What you need
* a cardboard box, big enough to get inside
* a blanket, shawl, rug, cushions
* favourite toys and comforters
* a CD player and quiet music or songs

What you do
Two children could share this quiet experience. It's good for children who have been angry or frustrated.
1. Put the cardboard box on its side and cut or tear off the flaps, so the children can get in and out easily.
2. Help the children to make a snug den inside the box, using the blankets and cushions.
3. Encourage the children to crawl into the den with their personal comforters or favourite soft toys.
4. Sing some quiet, soothing songs, or play some soft music as the children make a nest inside the box. Stay with them as they rest and play quietly, talking about what they are doing and what they can see from their den.

another idea:
* Add a safe night light or torch to the den.

Ready for more?
* Practice singing lullabies and quiet songs as well as exciting ones!
* Encourage children to make these sorts of nests and dens in corners, boxes, on settees and under tables, so they can look out at the world from a safe place.

Individual needs

☼ Children with limited movement may love to be inside a big box. Cover the inside with foil, or hang shiny things from the roof of the box.

☼ Make sure children with autistic spectrum disorders have short experiences of being with other children in a quiet space, but stay with them.

Tiny Tip

❋ Store boxes flat, so you can offer this activity regularly. Make some with windows and doors, peepholes and little slots for posting.

Watch, listen, reflect

👁 Watch for children who need quiet time to get over high stimulation or extreme feelings of frustration or anger.

👁 Listen for the language children use in these quiet times.

👁 Watch how children begin to work together to arrange a simple den or nest. Listen to the way they talk to each other.

Working together

Parents could:

* get a box for a den at home.
* sit and snuggle with their children every day.
* find some soft, soothing music to play at bedtime.

Practitioners could:

* give parents ideas of cheap or free resources they can use for play.
* display a list of lullabies and bedtime songs.
* add some quiet music CDs to the toy library or loan collection.

Me and you

Being together

What are they learning?

are they
   coping with stress?
   working together?
   trying new things?
this leads to
   * self control
   * a sense of well-being

Me and you

Being together

Movers, shakers and players

Aspect:
A Healthy Child

Components:
Emotional wellbeing

168

Find the Sound
listening and looking

What you need
* make a tape of simple sounds from your setting (hand washing, children singing, bikes in the garden, the toilet flushing, door bell, bricks falling etc.)
* photos of the objects or events

What you do
This activity takes a bit of preparation, but the game can be played over and over again with children at different ages.
1. Collect a small group of two or three children.
2. Say that you are going to play a listening and looking game.
3. Play the first sound, then stop and ask if they know what it is. Continue until you have played two or three sounds (not too many to start with). Stop after each one to talk.
4. Now spread out the photos on the table or floor. Look at them and name the activity or object on each.
5. Now play the sounds again, pausing after each to see if they can find the right picture for each sound.

another idea:
* Increase the number of sounds in the game as they get better at listening.

Ready for more?
🖐 Go on regular listening walks in the garden, in your setting or in the local area. Go with small groups of children, and start when they are babies.
🖐 Leave the game out sometimes for older children to play on their own.

Individual needs

☼ Try the game with one or two musical instruments and their photos.
☼ Make tapes of familiar people saying the child's name or a greeting. Add photos and watch for recognition.
☼ Use auditory clues to introduce regular activities - a little bell for snack time, a shaker for outside time.

Tiny Tip

✲ Some children are very sensitive to sounds and noises. Make sure you use sound and music regularly in your setting.

Watch, listen, reflect

👁 Watch for children who can really listen and discriminate sounds, and those who can't.
👁 Note the children who seem to respond well to music and sound. Use this to gain and maintain their attention.
👁 Watch for children who are very sensitive to sounds and loud noises. Discuss this with their parents.

Working together

Parents could:

* play simple listening games with their children.
* sometimes switch off the TV and radio, and have a quiet time with their children.

Practitioners could:

* talk to parents about the importance of listening skills to later learning and social development.
* encourage singing, nursery rhymes and music of all sorts.

Me and you

Being together

What are they learning?

are they
   listening?
   noticing differ-
   ences in sounds?
   matching sounds
   to objects?
this leads to
   * sound
     discrimination
   * listening

169

Resources for all stages of A Healthy Child

Things to collect

Contrasting black & white toys & pictures

Photos and pictures of faces and expressions, including those of the children and adults in your setting

Pictures of situations for discussion of safety and risk

Textured fabrics

Fabrics for parachute games and swinging

Fabrics to make tents and shelters

Shawls, blankets and snuggly materials

Big sheets of fabrics to use for hiding and finding games

Hats, scarves and gloves of all types, sizes and materials

Baby clothes for big dolls

Baby items - bottles, small disposable nappies, clothes, hats, toys, toiletries

Night & day clothes for teddies & dolls

Children's safety goggles, hard hats, crash helmets

Small beds, cots or boxes and bedclothes

Bracelets and bangles

Hair brushes and scrunchies

Ribbons

Baby safety mirrors

Stickers

Bells, rattles

Flannels and sponges

Soft toys and other objects to use for turn taking in circle time

Cardboard boxes and tubes, all sizes and shapes

Balls of all sizes & textures

Hoops, rings and quoits

Pictures from magazines and catalogues

Torches and battery lights

Natural & everyday objects for treasure and exploration baskets

Shallow baskets and trays

Small empty containers, ice cube trays, small yogurt pots

Spoons of all sizes

Straws

Paper and plastic plates

Small-world people, animals, vehicles.

Small world playground, park, street, etc

Small world and child size safety signs and notices

Road Safety signs, zebra crossings, traffic lights

Role play doctor's and dentist's kits

First aid equipment, bandages, doctors' coats

Wallpaper, wrapping paper, tissue, masking tape

Baby oil for massage (check for allergies before using nut oils)

CDs of soothing music, mobiles.

Toy telephones, (both 'mobiles' and others)

Simple tape recorder

Stories about feelings of happiness, loss, loneliness, jo expectation etc.

Books and stories

Title	Author	Publisher
The Little Book of Parachute Play	Clare Beswick	Featherstone Education
The Little Book of Light & Shadow	Linda Thornton & Pat Brunton	Featherstone Education
The Little Book of Circle Time	Dawn Roper	Featherstone Education
Be Safe	The Association for Science Education from www.ase.org.uk (Safety advice for nursery and primary schools and settings)	
Road Safety Guidance	(from your local authority)	
This Little Puffin	has a whole section of baby songs and rhymes	

Collect some books about childhood fears and anxieties, and add some which emphasise security and safety.
* Fact books and stories about first experiences of visiting the dentist, the doctor, being in hospital, having a new baby, going away to stay, etc.
* Books about visits and family experiences, including celebrations, happy events, parties, etc.
* Books about families and feeling safe, bedtime and being looked after
* Stories about night time, monsters, dinosaurs, getting lost and other frightening experiences, so children can 'practice being scared' in a safe environment.
You could ask your local librarian for suggestions of new and well loved titles - they may be prepared to lend some to your setting.

Brushes and rollers
Buy:
* decorators' brushes and rollers from DIY stores
* pastry brushes and pastry cutting rollers from cookshops
* baby hairbrushes from baby shops
* nail brushes and toothbrushes
* dishwashing and cleaning brushes from bargain shops
* craft rollers from art shops

Very small things
Try:
* 'hundreds and thousands' and sugar strands from the cake making bit of the supermarket
* pasta stars and shapes

Cardboard tubes
Try:
* carpet shops
* fabric shops
* packing & office suppliers
* printers

For Snack Time
* plastic plates and beakers (IKEA is good value)
* small plastic jugs (check that they pour well)
* spoons for serving (look for ones with chunky handles)
* small knives for cutting fruit, bread, etc (butter knives are good)
* plastic or fabric tablecloths

	Stage 1 0-8 months	Stage 2 8-18 months	Stage 3 18-24 months	Stage 4 24-36 months
A Strong Child	**Me, Myself & I;** (Purple pages from: 'I Like You, You Like Me')	**Being Acknowledged & Affirmed** (Purple pages from: 'Look At Me')	**Developing Self Assurance** (Purple pages from: 'I Can Do It')	**A Sense of Belonging** (Purple pages from: 'Me & My World')
A Skilful Communicator	**Being Together** (Pink pages from: 'What I Really Want)	**Finding a Voice** (Pink pages from: 'What's That?')	**Listening & Responding** (Pink pages from: 'Let's Listen)	**Making Meaning** (Pink pages from: 'Get the Message)
A Competent Learner	**Being Imaginative;** (Green pages from: 'Touch It, Feel It)	**Making Connections** (Green pages from: 'Count With Me)	**Representing** (Green pages from: 'Make Your Mark)	**Being Creative** (Green pages from: 'Let's Explore)
A Healthy Child	**Growing & Developing** (Blue pages from: 'Grab & Let Go)	**Keeping Safe** (Blue pages from: 'Tickle & Tumble)	**Making Healthy Choices** (Blue pages from: 'Which One?')	**Emotional Wellbeing** (Blue pages from: 'Me & You)

All four books in this series, and the 16 original Little Baby Books are available direct from the publisher, or from your usual book supplier. Special rates are available for bulk purchases.
Please phone for details on 01858 881212